DISCOVERIN

Discovering Pembrokeshire by Bicycle

JOHN FENNA

GOMER

First impression—2000

ISBN 1 85902 768 7

Printed in Wales at
Gomer Press, Llandysul, Ceredigion SA44 4QL

Contents

Acknowledgements

I would like to thank everyone, and particularly those acknowledged below, who helped me in producing this book which has been compiled in accordance with the 'Guidelines for Writers of Path Guides', produced by the Outdoor Writers Guild:

the Ordnance Survey, especially Steven Yates, without whose maps the rides could not have been attempted.

—Anthony Richards, the Pembrokeshire Coast National Park Access Officer; Jeremy George, Steward to the Barony of Cemais; Jonathan Hughes and Richard Elis, National Trust Head Wardens; Steve Stockham of the Preseli Cycle Group; Ms D. Griffith-Jones of SPARC; Ms S. Henehan of Menter Preseli; Mr D. Judd of Sustrans and Mr C. Dale of Pembrokeshire County Council, who checked that the routes described would not cause any problems, corrected small errors in the first draft, and provided additional information.

—Hazel Jones for reading and correcting the typescript and proofs.

—Alan Bradley for his excellent maps.

—and last, but far from least, my wife, Lis, who has not only typed most of this work but generally does all my typing, correcting, accounts, cooking, cleaning, gardening, ironing, photocopying, etc., as well as holding down a full-time job!

Introduction

The Pembrokeshire countryside and coastline offers a variety of scenery, from sand dunes and towering sea cliffs to moorland and crags; rolling farmland and deep wooded valleys to river gorges and tidal marshes. All of these various landscapes offer superb cycling and the choice of different scenery in a small area. It is hardly surprising that a large part of the most attractive landscape in the county forms the Pembrokeshire Coast National Park, which includes not only most of the county's coastline but also the Presely Hills and other inland areas. The park authority do a sterling job in maintaining and waymarking the footpaths and bridle-ways so that visitors can enjoy the magnificent Pembrokeshire countryside.

Man has left his mark on the landscape in a variety of ways. Prehistoric features such as burial chambers, cairns, hill-forts, standing stones and hut circles are found in abundance. The Presely Hills are famous as the source of many of the Stonehenge 'bluestones', and ancient legends recall that the area is also associated with the lives of Celtic saints, the exploits of King Arthur and one or two giants.

More recent signs of man's influence on the area are Roman, Celtic and Norman remains as well as disused quarries, old railway lines and old 'green roads', while the present rural landscape is the product of changing farm practices.

Pembrokeshire is famous for its wealth of wild flowers, some of which are rare. A variety of habitats support an abundance of species. During the spring and early summer the coastal cliffs are a riot of colour, and in autumn the hills are ablaze with the combined glory of gorse and heather.

The wide range of habitats are also home to a great variety of birds. The coast is a haven for sea birds, including the clown-like puffin, while various birds of prey, notably the buzzard, but also kestrels and peregrines, will be seen patrolling the hills.

Mammals are also seen in great variety, from dolphins and seals in the bays (seal pups are a charming addition to the rocky coves when new born and nearly helpless), to badgers and foxes which are seen in most parts of the county. Roaming on the hills you will find many ponies and sheep, while Welsh Black cattle will be found on many farms.

When out cycling, I would recommend you carry good field guides to bird, mammal and plant life identification (Collins Gem Books are excellent), and a pair of binoculars.

The appropriate OS maps are listed for each route. As well as helping you find your way, these fascinating documents can tell you much about the area in which the cycle ride is set. In addition to a map, a compass—providing you know how to use it—will also help to prevent you from getting temporarily 'lost' whilst out riding.

I have done my best to ensure that all the rides described are on public rights of way, or where the prior permission of the landowner has been obtained. Please keep to the route described, and when off-road follow the Off-road Cycling Code at all times.

It should be noted that, at times, the route described does not follow the exact paths shown on the Ordnance Survey maps. This can be explained by various factors including 'common usage' and locally agreed diversions, permissive paths and, in open country, agreed access. Errors on the maps are rare.

Occasionally, paths will change and if a new diversion is in place the route may differ from that shown on the map or described in the text. Recently diverted paths will invariably be well signposted.

Remember that some paths will also have other user rights: on bridle-ways you can expect to meet horses and walkers, as well as other cyclists, while you may meet vehicles on some 'green lanes'.

Should you encounter a problem in following any of the routes due to an unreasonable diversion or obstruction of a right of way, you are advised to send full details (including grid references) to the Welsh Officer of the Ramblers Association, Tŷ'r Cerddwyr, High Street, Gresford, Wrexham LL12 8PT (Tel. 01978 855148) and to the Access Officer of the Pembrokeshire Coast National Park Authority (Tel. 01437 775210) for problems inside the national park, or

Pembrokeshire County Council's Public Rights of Way Officer (Tel. 01437 775370) for problems outside the national park.

The times and distances quoted in this book are approximations only. The quoted times allow for a lack of total fitness, a difference of age, and pauses to explore points of interest along the way.

To cater for those cyclists who use miles and those who prefer kilometres, I have included both measurements in this book. To convert to your favoured system use the following conversion chart:

Yards		*Metres*
1.0936	1	0.9144

Miles		*Kilometres*
0.62137	1	1.6093

I strongly advise cyclists, whatever the time of year, to carry a full set of waterproofs, some extra food and warm clothing, a small first-aid kit and a survival bag, as a minimum, in case of emergency. This is especially important when cycling in remote areas.

Some of the routes follow paths close to natural and man-made hazards such as cliff edges, river banks and quarries. At such locations, particular care is necessary—especially if you have children with you—if accidents are to be avoided.

Finally, I hope that this collection of rides encourages locals and visitors alike to explore and enjoy the superb scenery of Pembrokeshire with the aid of the healthiest, cheapest and (in my opinion at least) one of the most pleasurable modes of transport—the bicycle!

The Off-road Cycling Code

Stay on the trail—either public bridle-ways or byways, **not** footpaths which are for walkers only.

Plan your route carefully—use the Ordnance Survey maps and check your route against the path 'key'.

Be courteous and considerate—always give way to walkers and horse riders, even if it means dismounting and lifting your bike out of the way.

Learn to prevent skids—and ride with control to prevent erosion, especially in the wet.

Keep to the paths—cycling on other tracks or on open ground is not allowed without permission from the landowner.

Be prepared—routes are shared with vehicles which should give way to cyclists, but may not expect you. So beware!

Give warning—your approach, especially from behind, can be almost silent and may startle other road users.

Moderate your speed—any form of racing on public highways, including bridle-ways and byways, is illegal.

Be safe—take food, a whistle and compass. Wear a helmet and carry waterproofs and spare clothing.

Be tidy—follow the Country Code.

Take a pride in your bike—make sure it is safe to ride, learn basic maintenance and take essential spares (puncture repair kit, pump, etc.).

Always treat it as a privilege to be able to ride across someone else's land. In that way an atmosphere of co-operation, not confrontation, can be forged.

The Country Code

Guard against all risk of fire

Fasten all gates

Keep dogs under proper control

Avoid damaging fences, hedges and walls

Keep to paths across farmland

Leave no litter

Safeguard water supplies

Protect wildlife, wild plants and trees

Go carefully on country roads

Respect the life of the countryside

The Grey Seal Code of Conduct
Extract from the Dyfed Wildlife Trust's Code

If you come across a seal on a beach: withdraw immediately and leave it alone. Do not fuss around the pup—the mother will probably be watching anxiously from the safety of the waves, and may abandon the pup if humans are in the vicinity. Do not let other people disturb the pup. Keep dogs well away. Do not move or handle the pup, drive it off the beach, try to get it into the sea, feed it, or try to take it home. Seals can give a very nasty bite.

If you think the pup has been abandoned: retire and observe from a distance (preferably down-wind) to see if the mother returns, and keep others from disturbing the pup. If the mother does not return within 4 hours, call the RSPCA/Dyfed Wildlife Trust Seal Network.

If the pup is obviously sick or injured: call the RSPCA/ Dyfed Wildlife Trust Seal Network immediately on 01990 555999. Do not try to move it or care for it yourself. If you find a dead seal, do not handle it as it may carry infectious diseases. Call the Strandings Line immediately on 01348 875000.

PLEASE

AVOID DISTURBING WILDLIFE

DO NOT PICK FLOWERS

TAKE YOUR RUBBISH—AND ANY YOU FIND—
HOME WITH YOU

TAKE ONLY PHOTOGRAPHS—
LEAVE ONLY TYRE TRACKS

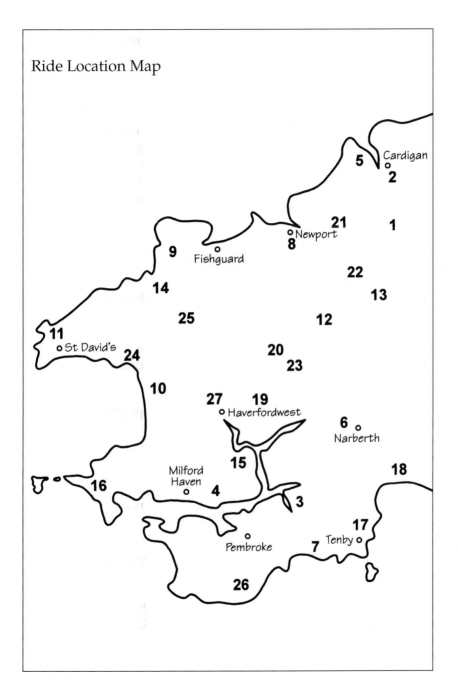

Ride Location Map

5 Cardigan ○ **2**

21 ○ Newport **8** **1**

9 ○ Fishguard **22**

14 **13**

25 **12**

11 ○ St David's **24** **20** **23**

10

27 **19** ○ Haverfordwest **6** ○ Narberth

15

Milford Haven ○ **4** **18**

16 **3** **17** Tenby ○

Pembroke ○ **7**

26

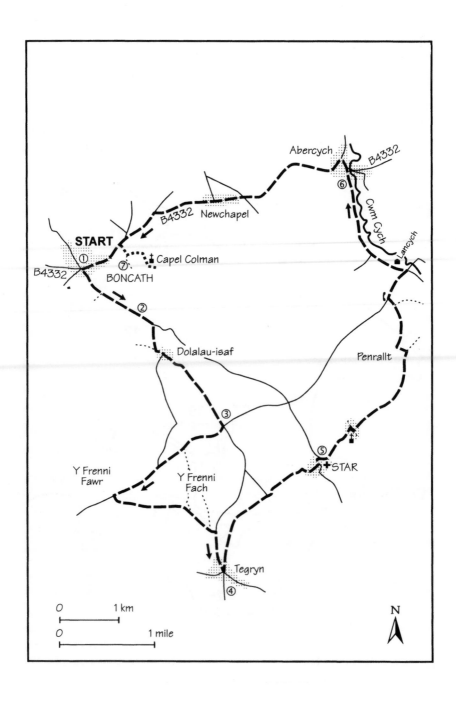

1 Boncath, Star and Cwm Cych

Fact File

Distance:	14½ miles (23.3 km)
Time:	4 hours
Maps:	OS Landranger 145 Cardigan & Mynydd Preseli; OS Pathfinder 1034 Boncath, Capel Iwan and Rhos
Start:	Boncath SN 204383
Nearest Town:	Cardigan
Terrain:	Quiet lanes and B roads. Some quite long and strenuous hills and short, sharp climbs, together with some long downhill runs (where you can rest your legs and catch your breath).
Refreshments:	Boncath: Boncath Inn and shop Tegryn: Butchers Arms Abercych: Nags Head Inn Newchapel: Ffynone Arms
Parking:	Limited roadside parking in Boncath
Suitable for:	Those families with enough stamina to cope with the uphill sections.

Along the way

This ride takes you along lanes in the north-west corner of Pembrokeshire, over the flanks of two prominent hills— Y Frenni Fach and Y Frenni Fawr—through quiet hamlets and down into the Cych valley, forming the Carmarthenshire/ Pembrokeshire border.

Several chapels and two churches are passed *en route*, and two mansions serve to remind us of the heyday of large estates.

The village of Boncath is named after the Welsh word for a buzzard, a relatively common bird of prey in the vicinity. South of Boncath, the summits of Y Frenni Fach and Y Frenni Fawr, as well as providing stunning views, are both sites of ancient tumuli. The Bronze Age cairns on Y Frenni Fawr, said to hold a lead chest filled with gold, are protected by a storm-bringing phantom, and guardian fairies, the *Tylwyth Teg*.

One of the ancient Welsh legends in *The Mabinogion*, regarded as a masterpiece of medieval European literature, recalls that Cwm Cych is one of the entrances into the underworld and on a dark winter's evening, when the bare branches of the trees stand stark against the sky and icicles hang from the roadside rocks,the imagination can often run riot in this noble, tree-girt valley.

In addition to the entrance to the Other World of the Celts, Cwm Cych is the site of a fascinating house, Lancych Mansion. The original house, built in the 16th century, was bought by the current owner's great-great-great-grandfather in the 18th century. The building was remodelled in 1820 and today it remains much as it was early in the 19th century. This wonderful private house holds a vast collection of medical reference books (one of only twenty private libraries still existing in Wales), and three ghosts. One ghost is said to be a monk from a monastery that supposedly stood here in the Middle Ages; another is a child chased by hounds alongside the river; and the third, a Jack Russell terrier!

The Nags Head Inn at Abercych is also home to spirits—of the bottled kind! However, the inn is more famous for its own next-door brewery and huge collection of bottled beers, as well as good food.

The entrance of the driveway leading to Cilwendeg is also passed *en route*. This magnificant mansion, built with the revenue from the last privately-owned lighthouse in England and Wales, was owned by William Trench, whose offspring built the original house. The lighthouse, situated off Anglesey, was eventually bought by the government in 1841 for nearly £445,000, a huge sum in those days. In the 1780s Cilwendeg was transformed into a Georgian mansion and was owned by several families before being requisitioned by the government during the Second World War to house staff of the Projectile Development Establishment, based at Aber-porth, and then for use by the Women's Land Army. Now owned by Pembrokeshire County Council, Cilwendeg is a residential home for the elderly. Like Lancych, it is said to be haunted, this time by a lady with a cough, wearing a long dress and skull cap.

Near Cilwendeg, off-route but worth a detour, is Capel Colman Church and standing stone inscribed with crosses. Anyone interested in ley lines will recognise the name Colman as one associated with leys. The combination of church and standing stone is another feature of leys.

Much of the route offers superb views but be warned—you have to suffer the climbs up to the high points. But at least you can then free-wheel down into the valleys!

Route

1. From Boncath head south down the road opposite the inn (note the stone buzzard over the door), signposted to Bwlchygroes, past the Post Office. This gives you an initial long, downhill run past a chapel and down to a bridge by an old mill with a chequered history.
2. Felin-wen, once a working corn mill, has also been a pottery and is now a factory producing a very superior range of jams and preserves.

   From the bridge, climb uphill for some 250 yards to the T-junction by Post-gwyn, turn right and follow the lane to the T-junction by Dolalau-isaf where you bear left and pass by a ruinous church half hidden on your left by a telephone box. At the next T-junction go straight ahead, following the sign to Tegryn, up a long (almost 1 mile) climb with views of the north-west slopes of Y Frenni Fawr to your right.
3. At the crossroads at the top of the hill, turn right, signposted to Crymych. After a short, stiff climb up the side of Y Frenni Fach, you are rewarded by an almost level, then downhill ride of over a mile (ignore the turn to the right) and superb views. At a T-junction at the foot of the southern slopes of Y Frenni Fawr, turn left towards Tegryn. The road takes you past Penlan-uchaf, down a quiet lane with excellent views and then gently up to a T-junction. At the Tegryn signpost, turn right and head into the village.
4. In Tegryn, turn sharp left at the crossroads just past the pub (opposite a petrol station) and head down a narrow lane

flanked by steep banks and high hedges with mature broadleaf trees, while grass sprouts in patches along the middle of the road. Keep straight on at the T-junction by Pen-banc and follow the lane steeply down to the hamlet of Star.

5. This quiet spot once boasted a corn and woollen mill, but is now little more than a collection of cottages and ruinous buildings on the floor and sides of Cwm Cneifa.

At the T-junction in the village, turn left and climb a steep zigzag up to a T-junction just above the Baptist chapel. At this junction the main road doubles back left, but our route goes right (or straight on, depending on how you look at it) and is signposted to Cwmcych.

At the old milk-churn stand and post box be sure to turn right, not left up a private track. This quiet winding lane, flanked by high hedges, zigzags past the dead-end road to Clydau parish church (St Clydias) perched above the floor of Cwm Cneifa.

A sharp zigzag by Penrallt takes you uphill before dropping down to a T-junction and telephone kiosk ¾ mile ahead. Turn right, signposted to Cwmcych, and descend steeply past a strawberry-pink house into the atmospheric Cwm Cych.

At the crossroads at the bottom of the hill, turn left, signposted to Abercych and head past Lancych Mansion as far as the road junction by the Nags Head Inn at Abercych. The village was once famous for its wood turners and clog makers.

6. Turn left at the junction, signposted B4332 and Boncath, and follow the road up and around a sharp bend left to climb the lung-crunching and leg-sapping 1¼ mile hill ahead. It is no disgrace to get off and push, occasionally turning to enjoy views of the Teifi and Cych valleys behind you.

Eventually you reach the crossroads near Newchapel— where it is said the last local hanging took place—before enjoying a short downhill ride through the village. The Ffynone Arms is a good place to recover from the stiff climb with the aid of a reviving drink!

Follow the B4332 back to Boncath, a mere 2 miles of gentle uphill and level cycling past an attractive house with a pond situated alongside a zigzag in the road, and the entrance to Cilwendeg Mansion.

7. A visit to Capel Colman Church, in order to see the standing stone and enjoy the views, is recommended for those with energy left. It adds only about half a mile to the route. To reach the church, turn left, signposted Capel Colman Church, about 100 yards past the entrance to Cilwendeg.

A sometimes strenuous ride, this route repays effort with some very enjoyable cycling and superb views.

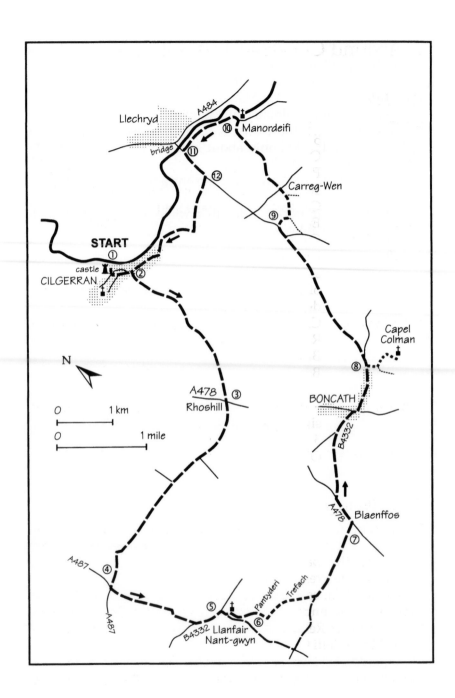

2 Around Cilgerran and Boncath

Fact File

Distance:	18 miles (28.9 km)
Time:	5 hours
Maps:	OS Landranger 145 Cardigan Mynydd Preseli; OS Pathfinder 1011 Newcastle Emlyn; 1034 Boncath, Capel Iwan and Rhos; 1010 Cardigan and Dinas Head
Start:	Entrance to Cilgerran Castle SN 194431
Nearest Town:	Cardigan
Terrain:	Undulating lanes and tracks with a short section on the busy A478. The initial climb out of Cilgerran is repaid later with free-wheeling descents.
Refreshments:	Cilgerran: many pubs and Castle Kitchen Restaurant for teas and coffee Blaenffos: shop Boncath: Boncath Inn and shop Llechryd: Carpenters Arms
Parking:	Car park by the river in Cilgerran. Follow signs 'To the river' by the Post Office.
Gates:	3
Suitable for:	Older children and stronger cyclists

Along the way

North Pembrokeshire is far more hilly than the southern part of the county and this ride has its fair share of ups and downs, rewarding the participant with superb views of the Teifi Valley and the Presely Hills.

The quiet lanes take you past several important historic sites; from the imposing ruin of Cilgerran Castle, at the start, to the scene of Rebecca Riots at Llechryd, and the quiet calm of old Manordeifi Church.

Cilgerran Castle, now in the care of Cadw, dates from 1223, though an earlier castle on the site was the scene of the

7

abduction of Nest, the Welsh Helen (the face that launched 1,000 coracles?) from her Norman husband by a Welsh prince. Standing high on a crag above the River Teifi, the castle provides spectacular views of the gorge. The site is well worth a visit, and should the gate be locked the key is available from the nearby shop.

The information panels by the toilets in the riverside car park give details of Cilgerran's past, while Cilgerran Church, nearby but off-route, is worth a visit. A 6th-century stone, with Ogam and Latin inscriptions still visible, is set amongst more recent gravestones on the south side of the church.

Other places of worship passed *en route* include the charming church at Llanfair Nant-gwyn, with its attractive stained glass, and Manordeifi Church. Both are worth stopping to admire but, of the two, Manordeifi is the most interesting. The present building dates from the 13th century, but there has possibly been a church here since AD 550. A fine example of the Celtic bellcote style, the church is unadorned and serene with many medieval features, including the bell made around 1450-1500. The font is Norman and the unusual box pews date from the 18th century. These box pews had individual features built into them by the families that owned them. Two at the east end have fireplaces, while those at the west end are decorated with fluted columns. The coracle in the porch is a reminder that the church is built on the Teifi floodplain and was used to ferry parishioners home—and rescue the prayer books—during times of flooding. The river has been known to flow through the building!

As well as churches and chapels, there are other places of interest where you can stop for a while and regain your breath. For example, at Llechryd a short stroll westward along the river from the 17th-century bridge takes you to the site of the old Penygored tinworks, and Y Gored, a fish weir destroyed by Rebecca rioters in 1843. The rioters, disguised as women and led by the mysterious and anonymous Rebecca, set about destroying unjust toll gates and other hindrances to free trade. By the weir stands an old ice house where the fish were once stored. Little remains of the old tinworks, though the canal used to supply water to the works runs parallel to the route for some distance between Manordeifi Church and Llechryd bridge. The silt-choked canal bed only holds water during times of flood.

For wildlife lovers, you will see much in the way of flowers and birds along the way.

Route

1. From Cilgerran Castle turn left by the Castle Kitchen Restaurant to join the road that runs through the village, now quiet and attractive but once an important market centre. Follow the main street for some 150 yards before turning right and heading south along a road signposted to Crymych and Tenby.
2. *En route* to the crossroads at Rhoshill, the road heads past the village sports ground and an imposing Welsh nonconformist chapel, Tŷ-rhos. There are extensive views over the Teifi Valley, to the north.
3. At Rhoshill, head straight across the busy A478 and follow the quiet lane signposted to Eglwyswrw. This winds its way across to the A487, providing superb views and passing some very attractive properties. Ignore all side turnings until you arrive at the main road by a group of cottages.
4. Rather than follow the main road, turn sharp left and head along a quiet lane signposted to Crymych and Cenarth, as far as the B4332, enjoying views of the Presely Hills as you go. Turn left at the T-junction and follow the road towards Cenarth for 200 yards, until you reach a second T-junction.
5. Turn right, signposted to Crymych, and follow the road for 150 yards as far as the gated lane by Llanfair Nant-gwyn Church, signposted Pantyderi Farm Manor, Family Holidays. Turn left to visit the church.
6. Continue along the lane, which, beyond Pantyderi, deteriorates into a rough track with two watersplashes and many puddles, turning right at track junctions once you leave tarmac until you reach tarmac again. After passing through Tre-fach farm, turn left at the T-junction at the end of the farm drive and head into Blaenffos.

For those who prefer to avoid rough tracks, return to the road after visiting the church and turn left. Continue southwards, over the bridge across Afon Nyfer and on to the crossroads. Turn left, signposted to Blaenffos, to rejoin the route described above at the entrance to Tre-fach farm drive.

7. On reaching the A478 at Blaenffos, turn left and follow the A478 north past the school and plant nurseries to the junction with the B4332, signposted to Boncath, Cenarth and Newcastle Emlyn. Turn right and head towards Boncath. Most of the climbing is now over and you can look forward to easy pedalling and free-wheel descents.

At the next T-junction, turn right and follow the B4332 through the village of Boncath, straight across the crossroads and on past the petrol station.

8. After leaving the village you have the option of visiting Capel Colman Church by taking the first turn to the right, signposted Capel Colman Church. The engraved standing stone is safely housed in the church.

Return to the B4332 and continue to the T-junction opposite the main entrance to Cilwendeg, signposted to Llechryd. Turn left and follow the lane with its flower- and bird-rich banks and hedges for some 1¾ miles to a junction where two lanes join from the right, just beyond a farm entrance and jewellery workshop. Take the second right turn, by a ruinous corrugated metal shed.

9. Head up this grass-centred and sometimes rather muddy lane, for a distance of 150 yards. Turn left at the T-junction ahead of you and follow the lane down to the crossroads at Carreg Wen. Go straight ahead, past the modern bungalows and down the lane alongside woods as far as the T-junction at Manordeifi.

10. Turn left to reach Manordeifi church, then head westwards, following the lane alongside the old canal to Llechryd bridge.

11. At the T-junction—after admiring the bridge, weir, ice house, etc.—head south away from the bridge (left at the junction, if you are not stopping), up past Castell Malgwyn and the entrance to Llechryd Cricket Club ground, on

your right, as far as the T-junction opposite a farm drive
and with an attractive house on the corner.
12. Turn right, signposted to Cilgerran, and along a pleasant,
tree-shaded lane above a winding stream to a T-junction,
with a telephone box. Turn right, again signposted to
Cilgerran, and follow the road past pleasant cottages,
situated above the old slate quarries, back into Cilgerran
and the start of your ride.

On the way into the village you pass (or not, as the case may
be!) two pubs: the Masons Arms (also known as the Ramp
Inn, as it is situated at the top of the old access ramp to the
quarries), and the Pendre Inn with its famous tree out in front.

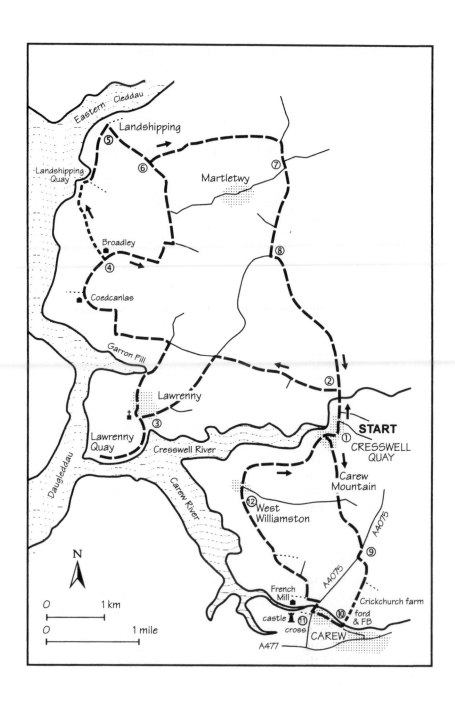

3 Around Cresswell and Carew

Fact File

Distance:	20 miles (32.1 km), or 15 miles (24.1 km) if the Carew section is omitted
Time:	4-5 hours for the full ride
Maps:	OS Landranger 158 Tenby & surrounding area; OS Outdoor Leisure 36 South Pembrokeshire
Start:	Cresswell Quay SN 050067
Nearest Town:	Pembroke
Terrain:	Rolling countryside with only a few short, steep climbs on mainly quiet lanes and tracks. The short off-road section near Landshipping can be made adventurous by venturing into deep mud and negotiating fallen trees in the woods. The ford near Carew may be impassable at times; on such occasions the footbridge is a blessing. The road at Garron Pill often floods at high tide, but a footbridge is available.
Refreshments:	Cresswell: Cresselly Arms Lawrenny Quay: Lawrenny Arms Hotel Lawrenny: Foreshore shop (seasonal tearooms) Landshipping: Stanley Arms Carew: Carew Arms, Riverside Restaurant and Tearooms
Parking:	Roadside parking at Cresswell Quay
Suitable for:	Family cycling

Along the way

This cycle ride takes you around the eastern side of the Daugleddau area, often known as 'the forgotten waterway'. It passes through charming villages on quiet lanes and tracks and takes you by several historic sites. Although much of the route is along high-hedged lanes you are rewarded with superb views of the quiet waters of the Daugleddau and the tidal Cresswell and Carew rivers.

13

Cresswell is said to take its name from the local well that was either holy (Christ's well) or gave a good crop of watercress. From the attractive old bridge to the north of Cresswell Quay you gain a good view of the picturesque ruins of the old castle.

Lawrenny once had a "castle" as well, a Victorian mansion, and although this has since been demolished, the church, one of the best preserved in the area, stands in what were once the "castle" grounds. The church, dedicated to the 12th-century Celtic saint Caradog, is well worth a visit as it contains some intriguing fittings and features.

Lawrenny Quay, although now quiet and used only by pleasure craft, was once a hive of industry, being a centre of ship-building, a port for the local coalmines and limestone quarries and, during the Second World War, a Royal Navy seaplane base.

Landshipping was also involved in coal and limestone shipping and the limekiln, now in a private garden, bears witness to past industry at this quiet quay.

Carew, at the southern end of this figure-of-eight ride, is probably the most intriguing spot visited during the day with some fine historic buildings and monuments to examine. Most notable is the castle, which dominates the Carew River. This site has been fortified since at least the Romano-British era (c.AD100-400), with the Normans adding a wooden motte and bailey castle. This structure was succeeded by a stone castle, which was added to and remodelled up until Elizabethan times (1530-92), with later fortifications being built and then destroyed during the Civil War.

In 1507 the castle hosted the last medieval tournament ever to be held in Wales with 600 Welsh gentry enjoying five days of jousting, banqueting and hunting. By the 1680s—suffering from the effects of the Civil War, when it changed hands four times, and slighted so as to reduce its worth to an enemy—Carew Castle had seen the last of its glory days and was abandoned. Now in the care of the Pembrokeshire Coast National Park Authority, Carew Castle is an attractive ruin to visit and is being restored with the help of Cadw: Welsh Historic Monuments.

Nearby, and also in the care of the National Park Authority, is the French Mill, which dates from the 18th century, but is on the site of a medieval mill. Carew Mill is the only surviving tidal mill in Wales, with water stored in the mill pond at high tide driving the mill machinery. Although it can only be reached on foot, the mill is well worth a visit.

The stone cross by the roadside in the castle grounds is one of the three finest Celtic crosses in Wales. With a Latin inscription which reads 'Maredudd the King, son of Edwin', the cross is a monument to Maredudd ab Edwin who with his brother Hywel ab Edwin became joint rulers of Deheubarth (the kingdom of south-west Wales) in 1033. Maredudd, however, died in battle two years later. The cross was made in two sections and the patterning is mainly Celtic, but shows, according to some experts, a Scandinavian influence.

Carew also boasts an intriguing Flemish chimney, now standing isolated by the road some 50 yards from the Carew Inn. The round, tapering chimney, set on a square base that includes a doorway and two ovens, was probably built in the 17th century, as was the attractive bridge over the Carew River.

Agriculture, mostly dairy farming and sheep grazing, is now the major industry in this part of Pembrokeshire but the route also takes you past the entrances to Tything Barn, once an oyster farm, and Cwm Deri Vineyard.

The more observant will not only note the variety of flora and fauna along the way but also spot some antique enamel disc AA road signs, as you follow the route from Cresswell Quay to Carew.

Route

1. From Cresswell Quay take the road north over Cresswell bridge and at the T-junction, within approximately 150 yards, bear left to Lawrenny.
2. The lane is steep and deeply sunken to start with but soon levels out, giving easy cycling to a crossroads where you turn left (signposted to Lawrenny) and head down another lane that leads to Lawrenny village.
3. In the centre of this attractive village, turn left and follow the foreshore road (signposted to Lawrenny Quay) to the Quay, before returning along the same route to Lawrenny.

   At the T-junction in the village, turn left past the entrance to the church and castle grounds. This quiet road takes you down to the head of Garron Pill, where the road is liable to flooding at high tide, and then climbs gently to a crossroads. Turn left and follow the undulating road past the ruins of St Mary's Church, in the first dip, and Coedcanlas, in the second. Dick Francis, the author, used to live here. At the T-junction just beyond Coedcanlas farm go straight ahead, climbing over a small hill before descending towards Broadley farm.

4. Just before the farm, at the start of some zigzags in the road, you can *either* undertake some off-road work, *or* stay on the surfaced road.

   If you choose to stay 'on road', continue along the road turning left at the first and second T-junction you encounter. At the third (6, see map), alongside which is a telephone box, turn right, signposted to Cross Hands, to rejoin the main route. This alternative route has several short, sharp climbs.

   If you prefer to follow the main route 'off-road', go left through the gate a little way short of Broadley farm. The initial green lane leads you into a field. Follow the right-hand boundary for some 250 yards, as far as a gate with a waymark. Turn right through the gate and follow the right-hand hedge around two sides of the field, down to a hunters gate which leads into the woods. Follow the waymarked rough path through the woods down to a lane where you turn right and head for Landshipping Quay.

5. From the quay, follow the road past the Stanley Arms up to a T-junction with a telephone box. Turn left, signposted to Cross Hands, and join the alternative road route.

   Between Broadley and Landshipping Quay the going can get very muddy and in the woods you may have to contend with fallen trees and muddy stream crossings, but you are rewarded with superb views of the Daugleddau and the Eastern and Western Cleddau rivers.

6. From the T-junction, where the two routes join, follow the quiet road for approximately 1¼ miles up to a T-junction where you turn right, signposted to Martletwy, Lawrenny and Cresswell Quay. Within about 250 yards there is another T-junction and you again turn right. At a third T-junction, by Cross Pottery and Sculpture, go straight on (left), signposted to Lawrenny and Cwm Deri Vineyard.

7. Follow the road for approximately one mile, passing the

T-junction which leads to the Vineyard, to a T-junction where you turn left, signposted to Cresswell Quay and Carew.

8. You now have a two mile run (ignoring any turn-offs) back to Cresswell Bridge and the start of the route at Cresswell Quay. Here you can either stop or continue for another 5 miles, taking in Carew.

If you decide to continue, follow the road past the Cresselly Arms, signposted to Carew, and, ignoring the T-junction as you zigzag out of the village, climb up and over Carew Mountain. This is not as hard as its name implies and within about 1½ miles, after having crossed over two minor crossroads, you reach the A4075.

9. At the T-junction, turn right, signposted to Pembroke. Taking great care, follow the road for approximately 150 yards before turning left by a roadside bungalow. Follow the lane —passing a sign for a ford and ignoring the turn to the left to a farmhouse B&B—and descend past Crickchurch Farm, where the lane becomes a rough track, as far as the ford.

10. If you do not fancy your chances in the water, wheel your bike over the footbridge to the far side where the track leads up to a surfaced lane.

Turn right to enter Carew village, past the Flemish chimney.

11. At the T-junction by the Carew Arms you will see the castle directly ahead, the Celtic cross to your left, and the tearooms and bridge to your right.

The route continues over the bridge, then left along the riverside road, signposted to West Williamston, giving superb views of both Carew Castle and French Mill. Follow the lane for about 1½ miles—past a picnic site, bearing left but heading straight on at a T-junction and passing the entrance to the old oyster farm—to reach West Williamston. *En route* are tantalising views over the Carew River, glimpsed through high hedges.

12. At the crossroads, with a telephone box, in the village, head straight on along a quiet lane, signposted to Cresswell Quay, that runs parallel to the Cresswell River. There is one steep climb before you arrive at the T-junction above Cresswell Quay. Turn left to return to the start of the ride in Cresswell Quay.

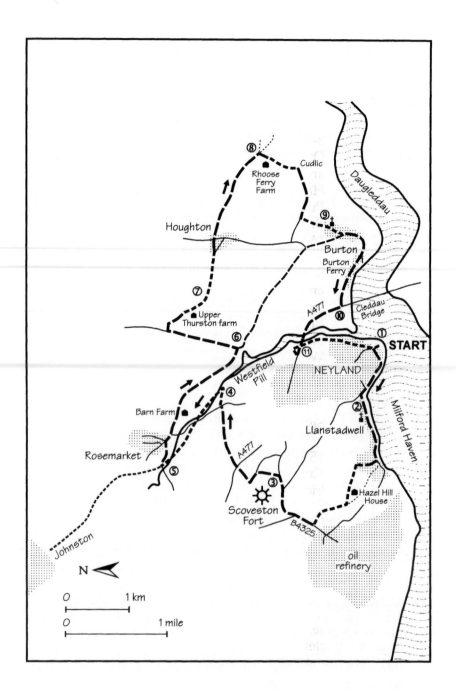

START

Daugleddau

Cudlic

⑧

Rhoose
Ferry
Farm

⑨

Burton

Houghton

Burton
Ferry

⑦

A4TI

Cleddau
Bridge

Upper
Thurston farm

⑩

①

⑥

Westfield
Pill

⑪

NEYLAND

Barn Farm

④

Llanstadwell

②

A477

Rosemarket

⑤

③

Hazel Hill
House

Johnston

☀
Scoveston
Fort

B4325

oil
refinery

Milford Haven

N

0   1 km

0   1 mile

4 Brunel Cycle Route

Fact File

Distance:	14 miles (22.5 km) or 17½ miles (28.1 km)
Time:	3-4 hours
Maps:	OS Landranger 158 Tenby & surrounding area; OS Landranger 157 St Davids and Haverfordwest; OS Outdoor Leisure 26 South Pembrokeshire
Start:	Brunel Quay car park SN 967048
Nearest Towns:	Milford Haven and Pembroke Dock
Terrain:	Mainly quiet lanes and bridle-ways through rolling countryside. Some short, steep climbs and one very steep descent. Muddy in places. Approx. 4 mile off-road (not including the Rosemarket option). Good waymarking.
Refreshments:	Neyland: shops, pubs, cafes, etc. Westfield Pill Marina: shop and cafe Rosemarket: Huntsman pub Burton Ferry: The Jolly Sailor pub Burton: The Stable Inn
Parking:	See Start
Gates and 'Bike Stiles':	15—many gates are to be found open
Suitable for:	Family cycling, but not with narrow-wheeled bicycles

My thanks to Menter Preseli for their help in producing this account. For more information on Menter Preseli's work, Tel: 01437 767655.

Along the way

The Brunel Cycle Route is a 14 mile circular route devised, waymarked, leafleted and, in places, surfaced and bridged by a project coordinated by Menter Preseli, and with the aid of funding from many agencies. The route takes in many sites of historical interest, not least those associated with Brunel's Great Western Railway with its terminus at Neyland. It was here that Isambard Kingdom Brunel (1806-59), the great Victorian engineer, hoped to establish an international port facility.

The route starts from Brunel Quay car park, by Westfield Pill Marina, where the area is landscaped and various information boards give a fairly detailed history of the locality. Various pieces of historic naval equipment decorate the area and some of Brunel's railway lines now do service as riverside fencing.

Originally, Neyland was a small fishing community, but in the 18th and 19th centuries Westfield Pill saw much shipbuilding in its sheltered water. For a short while there was a naval dockyard here but this was moved elsewhere due to the waterway being barely defensible in time of war.

The South Wales Railway Company bought the land around the original village and levelled it—including the village, which was rebuilt higher up the hill—in order to construct rail and port buildings. In 1859 the railway company also changed the name of the village to New Milford, although this later reverted to Neyland. Despite the fact that Brunel's plan for Neyland as an international liner terminal never came to fruition, Neyland was the terminal for the Irish ferry to Cork and Waterford until 1906. In 1914, however, the local fishmarket closed and in 1964 the last train ran from Neyland station. In 1975 the Cleddau Bridge opened, making the ferry over the Cleddau obsolete. Happily, the opening of the marina in 1985 restored Neyland's working connection with the sea, albeit for leisure purposes.

Upstream of the marina is the 13-acre Westfield Pill Nature Reserve, which incorporates some of the old GWR railbed. The site supports a wealth of flora and fauna and attracts otters, bats, reptiles and butterflies, as well as wading birds and many species of wildfowl.

Several small villages, linked by quiet lanes, are passed *en route* and these too have wonderful displays of wild flowers in season, and offer superb views of Milford Haven and the rolling countryside.

Llanstadwell, thought to have been settled sometime before Norman times, has a good anchorage. Medieval strip fields can be seen in the vicinity, while the attractive church has a rather unusual shape. Although a quiet village, Llanstadwell is dominated by the Gulf oil terminal built in the 1960s, while to the north of the industrial complex is Scoveston Fort, completed in 1865 to defend Milford Haven from the landward side. The fort is skirted by the cycle route but there is no public access to the building itself.

Rosemarket appears to be of Norman origin although it has a 5th-century church at its centre. Renowned in medieval days for its woollen cloth, Rosemarket was once more important than Haverfordwest and one of Charles II's mistresses was born in the village. The castle mound, south of the church, bears witness to the importance of this village in times past.

Houghton is also of medieval origin, with remnants of strip fields in the vicinity, while Burton is believed to lie in the main area of 12th-century English and Flemish settlements. Burton's 13th-century church has an interesting full-immersion baptistry, which is a restored holy well.

Westfield Pill used to be navigable as far as the lane below Westfield Hill farm, where there was a corn mill. Boats, used in the corn trade and for transporting limestone, could also carry items intended for Rosemarket. The mill, whose wheel was removed and replaced by a turbine in the 19th century, was in use up to the First World War.

A reservoir on top of the hill, which served Neyland station's steam trains' demand for boiler water, was filled by a coal-operated pumping station located near the mill. This finally closed in the 1950s and little now remains to be seen of any buildings, other than the old railway-crossing attendant's cottage which is now a private house.

Route

1. From the car park, regain the road and turn left, signposted to Milford Haven, and follow the waterside for approximately half a mile to the first left turn, signposted to Llanstadwell.

2. Turn left and follow Church Road for ¾ mile through Llanstadwell, past the attractive church, until you come to a T-junction. Turn right and follow the lane up-slope for approximately 200 yards, past the entrance to a housing estate, to a gate situated by a post box and bench.

   Turn left and follow a bridleway which zigzags across farmland, eventually gaining a wide green lane just beyond Hazel Hill House. This green lane brings you out onto the B4325, opposite school buildings. Turn right and follow the road towards Neyland, past a T-junction and down-slope of Scoveston Fort, which appears as a low mound of gorse and scrub on your left.

3. At the next T-junction turn left and follow the road signposted to Little Honeyborough and Unsuitable for Heavy Goods Vehicles, which makes it all the better for bicycles! After another 250 yards or so turn left again and head north along an even smaller lane below the east side of the fort. Here the views really open up and ahead you look out over rich farmland towards the Presely Hills in the distance. Do not look behind you unless you enjoy views of oil refineries and power cables!

   At the T-junction at the head of the lane turn left and follow the road round a sharp bend and down to the A477. Head over the main road—left, then immediately right—down a quiet lane to another staggered crossroads. On a bicycle, you can go straight over, across the grass, to enter the steep and winding lane that leads to Westfield Pill and the old railway crossing.

4. Turn left through the first of many examples of ingenious bike stiles. Known more properly as a Pembrokeshire Bicycle Gate it is designed to exclude motorbikes and horses, but to allow cyclists to follow the cycle trail. It has, as you could say, a 'stile' of its own!

Follow the old railway line through a delightful little valley. The surface is good and the valley is full of flowers, trees and the sound of the stream. At one point you cross a bridge over a road and, further on, pass below the remains of a hilltop fort, but both are hard to see through the trees.

5. Within a mile you come to a road where you have the choice of *either* crossing over and continuing along the railway to Johnston and back again, adding 3½ miles to your day, *or* turning right to follow the lane which climbs up to Rosemarket, cutting out the diversion altogether. Johnston was once a poor hamlet but, having grown during the railway era, is now a thriving village with its own station.

At the T-junction as you enter Rosemarket, turn right and proceed in a south-easterly direction. A short distance past Front Street, take the left turn signposted Unsuitable for Long Vehicles and follow the lane for approximately 1¼ miles, down across a stream and steeply up-slope past the very attractive Barn Farm, until you come to a wooded T-junction at the bottom of a steep hill.

6. Here you again have a choice: you can *either* turn right and follow the 'wet weather alternative' for about 1¾ miles to Burton, where it rejoins the main route by the Stable Inn, *or* head along the main route which turns left at the T-junction and climbs up for about ¾ mile to a right turn at a T-junction, marked as a bridle-way. Follow the surfaced lane past Upper Thurston Farm. Here it loses its surface and becomes a track. Continue along the track through the gardens of Lower Thurston Farm and up to some cottages where the track appears to end. Head between the front of the cottage and some outbuildings and through a gate leading into a green lane.

7. This section can be muddy in wet weather, despite some new wooden bridges over the streams and infill in the worst boggy patches—hence the 'wet weather alternative'! Beyond the worst section, by a bridle-way sign, you encounter a grass-centred track. Turn left and follow this pleasantly wooded track up to a T-junction with a surfaced lane at Houghton's village green. Turn left and continue

along the lane past the school up to a crossroads. Cross straight over and follow the dead-end Rhoose Ferry road ahead. Follow this lane for approximately 1 mile until you come to a multi-branched junction.

8. Take the right turn to Rhoose Ferry Farm and climb up to the farmyard, where the route loses its surface. Head straight through the farmyard and down a green lane, bearing right at a fork to the houses at Cudlic. Here you regain a surfaced lane which takes you west for about ¾ mile to a broad grass triangle, situated just before a house. Turn left and follow the green lane at the point of the triangle down to Burton.

9. At Burton Church bear right and head through the village to the T-junction near the Stable Inn where, joining up with the 'wet weather alternative', you turn left. Follow the road past an old toll house—erected in 1788, destroyed in 1843 and rebuilt at the cost of 3 shillings in 1844—and down towards Burton Ferry. Opposite the Jolly Sailor, turn right along a road signposted to Neyland and Milford Haven and climb up to the junction with the A477, where there is a picnic site and viewpoint at the northern end of the Cleddau Bridge.

10. Turning right onto the A477 and following it for approximately ¾ mile to the end of Westfield Pill Bridge demands great care, especially if you are with younger cyclists.

It is possible—just—to ride on the verge (it is planned to create a surfaced cycle track on the verge) until you reach the point where you have to re-cross the road, on the west side of Westfield Pill Bridge, where the waymark points you down a steep and loose path that doubles back on itself on the upstream side of the bridge.

11. Dismount and walk this section. At the bottom of the track you are, once again, on Brunel's railway line with the nature reserve on your left. Turn right, head under the bridge and follow the old line through the marina back to Brunel Quay and the start of the Brunel Cycle Route.

Brunel Quay, Neyland (Ride 4).

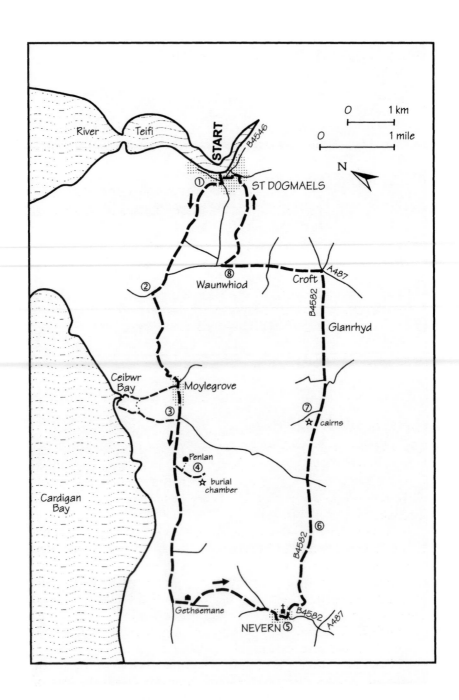

5 St Dogmaels and Nevern

Fact File

Distance:	17 miles (27.3 km) or 20 miles (32.1 km), depending on whether you take the recommended side trips
Time:	4-5 hours
Maps:	OS Landranger 145 Cardigan & Mynydd Preseli; OS Outdoor Leisure 35 North Pembrokeshire
Start:	St Dogmaels car park SN 165460
Nearest Towns:	Cardigan
Terrain:	Mainly on quiet lanes and the B4582, with a couple of steep climbs and descents.
Refreshments:	St Dogmaels: tearooms, pubs, shops, etc. Nevern: Trewern Arms
Parking:	See Start
Suitable for:	Families who have a bit of stamina for the hills.

Along the way

The route taken between St Dogmaels, on the shores of the Teifi estuary to the north-east, and Nevern, on the banks of the River Nyfer to the south-west, passes through some delightful scenery and links several sites of historic and prehistoric interest.

In St Dogmaels (the 'largest village in Wales') are the ruins of an abbey founded in 1115 by monks of the Norman, Tironensian Order. It was, at one time, the wealthiest monastery in Wales. Little is left to demonstrate its former wealth, though the mill (Y Felin), which was restored in the 1980s, may once have been abbey property. Y Felin (with an adjoining tearoom) is worth a visit and, with a mill having been recorded here since 1291, is of historic interest in its own right.

St Dogmael, after whom the village is named, was a Celtic saint who lived around AD 500. Further links with the 'age of saints' are to be found in the village church, which houses a memorial stone inscribed in both Latin and Ogam script, reading 'Sagranus, the son of Cunotamus'.

Nevern is also home to stones inscribed in both Latin and Ogam. The stone pillar beside the church door, called the Vitalianus stone, is inscribed 'Vitaliani Emereto' in Latin, 'the stone of Vitalianus, discharged with honour'. The Maglocunus stone, now embedded in a window sill inside the church, has a dual inscription reading 'the stone of Maglocunus, son of Clutorius'. The church, founded by St Brynach around AD 500-600 (though now of mainly Norman construction), has many interesting features including the south transeptal chapel with its stone vaulted ceiling. Stones in the outside walls of the church include a stone head (damaged) and one with a partial Latin inscription. Outside the church stands the famous, thirteen-foot Celtic cross erected about AD 1000, one of the most perfect of its kind. All four sides are heavily decorated with plaits, knots, frets and other patterns (note the mason's error on one leg of a swastika on a front panel) and bears two inscriptions: one probably an abbreviation of Dominus, but experts have failed to decipher the other.

The avenue of yews, contorted with age, are also famous because the second tree on the right from the church gate 'bleeds' a sticky red 'blood' at certain times of the year. This phenomenon has yet to be satisfactorily explained. Outside the gate is one of only two mounting blocks left in Pembrokeshire. According to the old Welsh wedding custom, it was used by a newly-wed wife to mount a horse in order to 'escape', 'pursued' by guests.

St Brynach, to whom the church is dedicated, is said to have communed with angels on nearby Carn Ingli, the 'Mountain of Angels', the prominent summit rising above Newport. According to legend, a stone on Carn Ingli, said to be the saint's pillow, will spin a compass needle right round!

The remains of Nevern Castle, built by Martin of Tours on the site of an Iron Age fort above the church in about 1094, are now mainly turf-covered and tree-grown with little stonework visible, although its broad outline with moat, dry ditch and inner motte, can easily be seen. In 1191 the castle was seized by Rhys ap Gruffydd, Henry II's 'right loving friend' and most powerful prince in south Wales. Today, however, Nevern is a quiet village. Newport, its near neighbour, is now much more important and was founded by Martin of Tours after the Welsh expelled him from Nevern!

Near the hairpin bend on the road between Nevern Castle and the village is a pilgrims cross cut in relief in the face of the rock, and smaller crosses are inscribed into the rock steps on the path believed to be the pilgrim route to St Davids. Legend also tells of a walled-up cave nearby containing the 'one true cross'.

The route also passes other antiquities including: a burial chamber on the hill south-west of Moylegrove; the site of an ancient settlement north-west of Moylegrove; a cup-marked rock; and Crugiau Cemais, three ancient cairns, and now the site of a striking viewpoint, above Glanrhyd.

Full of interest, this route follows quiet roads that, as well as giving good views, are often flanked by high-banked hedges, the home to a wide variety of fauna and flora. Naturally, to gain the views, you have some climbing to do (especially coming out of deep-set Moylegrove), but the downhill free-wheeling makes up for this—I hope.

Route

1. From the car park, turn right and climb up through the village, signposted to Moylegrove, on the first and rather long climb of the day. Follow the road to the right at the hairpin bend at Cwmins (signposted to Moylegrove and Newport), soon after which the angle of climb moderates. The views over the Teifi estuary are superb and, as you climb, widen to include Cardigan Bay and Cardigan Island. Follow this quiet lane for approximately 2½ miles, passing two T-junctions with roads coming in from the left.
2. At the third T-junction, turn left, signposted to Moylegrove, and enjoy a mainly downhill run, with superb coastal views, past an ancient settlement or fort and into Moylegrove. The last part of this section is steep and winding, so make sure your brakes are in good working order!

Ignore the road coming in from your left as you enter the village, cross the bridge and go straight ahead. By the chapel you have the option of extending the route by approximately 1½ miles by turning right, signposted to Ceibwr, to visit Ceibwr Bay, an attractive rocky inlet.

3. If you take this alternative route, you can rejoin the main route by following the road which heads southwards from Ceibwr, over a crossroads, as far as the T-junction half a mile south-west of Moylegrove. At the junction, turn right.

The main route heads straight through the village of Moylegrove and passes the school on a very steep climb (signposted to Newport), which moderates and becomes easier as you gain height.

Just over a mile beyond the village, you again have the option to extend the route by about 1 mile in order to visit the prehistoric burial chamber of Llech y Drybedd. You will be rewarded by some fantastic views of the Presely Hills, the Nyfer valley and along the coast.

4. To visit the burial chamber, turn left and follow the concrete drive of Penlan farm, ignoring the left turn to the farm itself. At a fork in the track beyond the turn to Penlan, bear left and within about 150 yards you will encounter a stile on the right. Cross the stile to reach the cromlech. Unfortunately, from road to cromlech there is only legal access on foot, so you should push your bike to the burial chamber and back.

Having taken in the views, retrace your steps and turn left. Follow the road up the last part of the rise before enjoying a pleasant downhill run towards the south-west. Ignore the first turn to the left, signposted to Nevern, and carry on along the road signposted to Newport Beach.

At the next T-junction, turn left, signposted to Gethsemane. A short distance past Tredrisi Fawr farm, bear left at the T-junction and enjoy a roller-coaster ride down quiet lanes. After about a mile, go straight on at the first T-junction and right at the next, which lies a short distance down-slope. This road takes you down into Nevern, past the castle and the sign, on a hairpin bend, to the Pilgrim's Cross.

5. At the T-junction in Nevern, turn left and follow the quiet B4582 for about 5 miles to Croft, ignoring all side roads.

6. *En route* you pass by some interesting sites, including some enigmatic prehistoric carvings or 'cup marks' on a rock in a field on your right, about 1¼ miles from the T-junction in Nevern. The site can be seen from the gate, just past a footpath, waymark and stile on your right.
7. Also to be seen (and I recommend a visit) are the three cairns of Crugiau Cemais at the top of the hill you have been climbing gradually since leaving Nevern. Access is by a gate on your left and up a grassy track. You will be rewarded by one of the best views of the day.

   On reaching the A487 at Croft, turn left (signposted to Cardigan) but leave the main road almost immediately, in favour of a much quieter road, by turning left again, signposted to Moylegrove. Follow the minor road for approximately 1½ miles, straight across a crossroads, as far as a T-junction on a sharp bend.
8. Turn right and enjoy a glorious downhill run through Cwm Degwel, a wooded, rocky gorge, back down into St Dogmaels.
9. At the T-junction by the old school buildings turn left to visit the abbey, church and mill, and then on to a T-junction almost opposite the car park from where you set off.

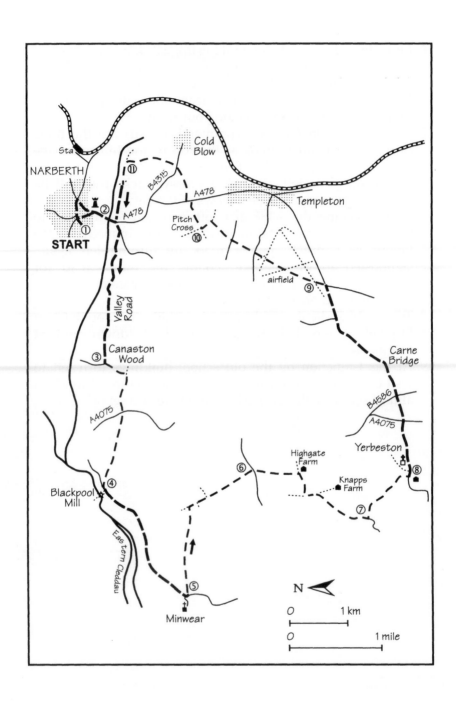

6 Narberth and Canaston Woods

Fact File

Distance:	16 miles (25.7 km) off-road on bridle paths and tracks
Time:	4-5 hours
Maps:	OS Landranger 158 Tenby & surrounding area; OS Outdoor Leisure 36 South Pembrokeshire; *Landsker Cycle Routes—Off Road Routes* (leaflet published by SPARC)
Start:	Narberth car park SN 108147
Nearest Towns:	Narberth
Terrain:	Well waymarked tracks, bridleways and minor roads. Can be muddy in places. Some stiff but short climbs; otherwise rolling countryside. Track hard to find over Templeton airfield.
Refreshments:	Narberth: pubs, shops, cafes, etc. Blackpool Mill: cafe
Parking:	See Start
Gates:	12
Suitable for:	Mountain bikers who enjoy a rural challenge

While researching a suitable cycle route for this part of Pembrokeshire, I came across this route waymarked by SPARC as part of The Greenways Project. One section, near Highgate Farm, is not a right of way, but access is permitted by the landowner, thanks to negotiations by SPARC. Do nothing to jeopardise this permission.

SPARC—South Pembrokeshire Partnership for Action with Rural Communities—is funded partly by Europe to help with rural initiatives, such as setting up this cycle route. For more information on SPARC Tel: 01834 860965.

Along the way

Narberth, a pleasant and quiet rural town sited on the Landsker, the border between the Welsh- and English-speaking areas of

Pembrokeshire, has at its centre an excellent visitor centre in the old Town Hall. But life was not always as peaceful here as it is now. The ruins of the Norman castle may be the site of the Court of Pwyll mentioned in *The Mabinogion*, the oldest recorded Welsh legends. In Pwyll's days Arberth was the capital of the Kingdom of Dyfed. In the more recent past Narberth was a centre for cattle droving and the scene of Rebecca Riots which began in west Wales in the summer of 1839. Those who were against paying exorbitant road tolls disguised themselves as women and set about destroying toll gates.

Blackpool Mill, situated on the Eastern Cleddau river, is on the site of an earlier mill first mentioned in 1555. It also included a 16th-century iron forge. The mill now houses an exhibition devoted to explaining the old milling processes and machinery, while the cellars have been converted to a series of 'caves' illustrating extinct prehistoric wild animals that once roamed the area: bears, hyenas, boar and reindeer, and even the famous Welsh Red Dragon!

Remains of a more modern kind, in the form of a now largely disused airfield, are encountered near Templeton. This once busy Second World War airfield is generally quiet but is still occasionally used for military exercises and motorcycle riding tests. The route also passes close to several ancient earthworks and castle mounds, indicating that warfare is not just a modern preoccupation.

Minwear was probably first settled by Viking raiders. In 1150 the church of St Womars, Minwear, was granted by Robert, son of Lomer, to the Knights of St John of Jerusalem Hospitallers who became a redoubtable fighting force during and after the Crusades. The fine church was originally a single chamber but by the 14th century several additions had been built, including the tower. Although extensively restored by Baron de Rutzen of Slebech in 1874, the original stonework is still visible in the nave and pillars. The font is not original but was found in a nearby farm, where it was used as a pig trough. The four faces are perhaps those of the evangelists.

En route is Oakwood, with its rides and attractions, Wales' answer to Alton Towers. As you pass by, ignore any screams you may hear—for they are only the sounds of people enjoying themselves being terrified on the roller-coaster! Quite a contrast to the quiet of most of this cycle ride!

This rural ride, which passes through delightful country-side, has enough to satisfy anyone looking for a bit of a challenge, without being too rugged. Along the high-hedged lanes and across woodland and field paths, the variety of wildlife encountered is immense: from buzzards to wrens, squirrels to badgers and a wealth of wild flowers—a naturalist's and cyclist's delight.

Route

1. From the entrance to the car park, turn right and join the one-way system, turning right again at the junction at the end of Spring Gardens, a site dominated by a modern version of a Celtic cross. Turn right here, signposted to the Town Centre and Tenby, and follow the road downhill, bearing left at the war memorial, to Narberth Bridge at the bottom of the hill, overlooked by the castle ruins.

2. A short distance beyond the 30 mph limit, turn right at the post box, signposted Heronsbrook Leisure Park. At the T-junction 50 yards ahead, turn right up Valley Road and follow this route for approximately 1½ miles to a point where the road turns sharp right and a track enters from the left.

3. Turn left and follow the track through the woods for about half a mile until it meets a broad, cross trackway. At first the track into the woods is deeply sunken and very muddy —too muddy to cycle, too narrow to push!—but widens and becomes a joy to ride.

   At the cross track, part of the Knight's Way Walk, turn right and follow this excellent route west for 1½ miles (take great care crossing the A4075) as far as the quiet, narrow road near Blackpool Mill.

4. Turn left, past Blackpool Mill (which you may choose to visit) and follow the road through Minwear Wood for some 1½ miles to a T-junction at Minwear. Turn right, signposted as a dead end, to visit the charming church, or

bear left. Then, almost immediately, leave the road and join the bridle path through a gate on your left.

5. This fun route, of about 1 mile of green lane, has a few muddy and overgrown sections, but is generally reasonably well surfaced and leads you to a junction with a farm lane. Turn right and follow the lane, past two farm entrances, until you meet the road about a mile further on.

6. At the junction, turn right. Follow this quiet road for a few yards only before turning left up a permissive path. This takes you up another green lane, along a field boundary and a continuation of the green lane, and down to a surfaced farm lane near Highgate farm.

   Turn right and follow the lane, which soon loses its surface to become a farm track, leading down to the entrance to Knapps Farm. Turn right and follow the track as it becomes rougher and more exciting, eventually being more like a green lane.

7. Some ¾ mile on from the turn by Knapps Farm, the track joins a surfaced lane again, but this is abandoned almost immediately as you turn sharp left up a green lane signposted as being Unsuitable for Motors. Within half a mile this lane joins a farm track which you follow straight on uphill to join a surfaced lane by Yerbeston Farm.

8. Turn left, past the derelict Yerbeston Church and follow the road across the A4075 and the B4586 (the road you are following is signposted to Templeton and Narberth). After dropping down to Carne Bridge and climbing steeply up the other side of the valley (the stream is somewhat confusingly named Loveston Lake, 'lake' being a common south Pembrokeshire word for a winding stream), continue along the main road to the T-junction (a minor road enters from the right) on the southern edge of the disused Templeton airfield. Here you abandon the road, taking the bridle path, half hidden in the hedge, from the small lay-by just beyond the road signs.

9. Although MoD signs exhort you to follow the bridleway which runs at a 45° angle from the hedge, diagonally across the first runways, in practice (at time of writing) this is difficult as the route is overgrown. If the bridleway is

not cleared soon, many people will probably take the 'easy option', by-passing the obstruction by following the runway to the right until they meet the north-south runway, following the north-south runway to its northern end, before turning right on the perimeter road, past one old dispersal bay, then left down a narrow surfaced trackway until they encounter MoD signs informing people to keep to the bridleway! However, I recommend you try to stick to the bridleway as this will help keep the legal right of way open.

Having eventually crossed the airfield, and the A4115, take the track which heads north between the cottages and a driveway. This leads into a green lane which climbs, often across bare rock, and crosses a narrow lane before terminating at a T-junction, where you turn left.

10. After a short section of zigzag track you reach Pitch Cross. At the crossroads of tracks, turn right and head down past two farms to reach the A478. Turn left, then almost immediately right down a farm track. This track, which passes one or two cottages, deteriorates into a green lane before dropping down to a crossing directly over the B4315 (north of aptly-named Cold Blow). The lane on the opposite side of the B4315 soon deteriorates into a farm track, then a green lane and eventually into a steep sunken lane, bounded by high banks, that takes you down into a wooded valley.

11. At the bottom of the slope lies a track junction centred on a large tree stump and roots. Turn left and follow the rather muddy green lane until it meets a surfaced farm lane. Turn right and follow the farm lane westwards, past a T-junction (near to which are Narberth Mill Ponds where you can use the bird hide, restored by SPARC, to observe wildlife), a holiday park and a business park, back to Narberth Bridge.

12. Turn right and climb the hill below the castle, up to the war memorial. From here follow the one-way system past the museum and visitor centre and through the centre of town. At the top of the road, turn left and left again to re-enter the car park.

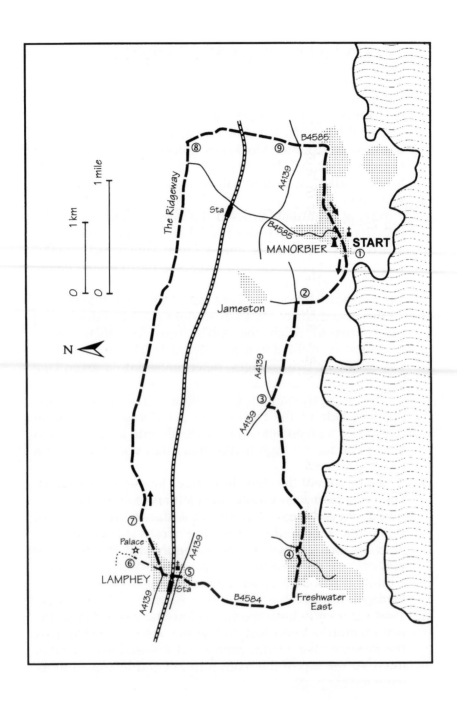

7 Around Manorbier and Lamphey

Fact File

Distance:	12½ miles (20.1 km)
Time:	3½ hours
Maps:	OS Landranger 158 Tenby & surrounding area; OS Outdoor Leisure 36 South Pembrokeshire; OS Pathfinder 1125 Manorbier and Tenby
Start:	Manorbier Beach car park SN 063976
Nearest Towns:	Tenby and Pembroke
Terrain:	Mainly on quiet lanes with very few steep hills; gentle undulations are the rule.
Refreshments:	Manorbier: Castle Inn, Castle Mead Hotel tearooms and gardens, cafe and shop Lydstep village: Lydstep Tavern Between Manorbier and Freshwater East: Swanlake Bay tearoom Lamphey: The Dial Inn
Parking:	See Start
Suitable for:	Family cycling

Along the way

On arriving at the start of the route you cannot help but notice the walls of Manorbier Castle towering above the car park. The castle, which has a fascinating history, is still a private residence and although the residential quarters are not open to the public, the delightful ruined sections and gardens are not to be missed.

The castle we see today was begun in the 12th century and was the baronial home of the de Barri family, who were granted these productive lands after military service during the Norman invasion of Ireland. The most famous member of the family was Giraldus Cambrensis—Gerald of Wales—one of the finest scholars of his day and a chronicler of notable events. There is no room here to recall the cleric's biography, though the excellent guide to the castle, available in the castle shop, records his life and selections from his writings.

After the Wars of the Roses, Manorbier became Crown property, but in 1670 the declining estate and castle were sold to Sir Erasmus Phillips of Picton Castle, from whom the present owner descends.

Never having suffered an all-out assault, the castle is in good repair, although alterations during the Civil War caused arrow slits to be blocked up or fitted with musket loops. When conflict did disturb the tranquility of the area it rarely touched the castle, mainly, it seems, due to political and family connections.

The house and gardens were renovated by J. R. Cobb in the 1880s, halting a serious decline and making the residence habitable again. More work was done under the supervision of Lady Dunsany and her son-in-law Francis Dashwood, Bart.

Also worth a visit, is the dovecote in the valley west of the castle, and Manorbier Church, dedicated to St James the Great, located south of the castle. Built on ancient foundations, the church shows evidence of many different periods of construction which have made it historically interesting and a delight to the eye. Details of its fascinating history and other features of the church are recorded in the guide written by John Farfield Davies. This publication, which is available in the church, covers many subjects of local interest—from prehistoric remains to 19th-century education.

In Lamphey both the church and the ruins of Lamphey Palace are worth visiting. The palace was once the luxurious rural retreat cum country house of the Welsh bishops of St Davids, the most powerful clergy in Wales. Here they could relax from the cares of their duties as royal ministers, baronial landlords and—yes, I nearly forget—church officials.

Added to by successive bishops between the 13th and 16th centuries, Lamphey Palace was the centre of an opulent estate with parkland, orchards, fishponds, brewhouse, bakehouse, banqueting halls, private apartments for the bishop and separate accommodation for staff and guests. There are even the remains of a chapel! Surrendered to the Devereux family during the reign of Henry VIII, this mighty palace is now a ruin in the care of Cadw and can be enjoyed by all, its peaceful setting an ideal spot for a break on the cycle route.

From Lamphey the route follows the Ridgeway back towards Manorbier. Judging by the number of tumuli along its length, the Ridgeway must be an ancient trackway of great significance. It was the link between Pembroke and Tenby until the A4139 was engineered in its shadow. Providing superb views, the Ridgeway is now a quiet backroad ideal for cycling, undulating and winding its way between hedgerows and attracting little traffic to disturb the peace of the countryside.

Rich in interest, this route also provides easy access to superb beaches, and is not over strenuous for those of average fitness.

Route

1. Leaving Manorbier Beach car park, turn left and follow the minor and very narrow road over the bridge spanning the stream that once supplied Manorbier castle with water, and up The Dak, one of the few steep climbs of the day, to more level ground landward of the coastal cliffs.
2. On reaching a crossroads, turn left, following a cycle route waymark in a westerly direction. Follow the road, past the drive to Swanlake Bay Farmhouse tearoom, as far as its junction with the main A4139.
3. Go straight ahead (left) for some 150 yards to a T-junction, where the main road is abandoned as you turn left down a lane signposted as unsuitable for motors. The lane, however, is very suitable for cycles and eventually heads past the Freshwater Inn (I hope the name does not refer to the drinks available!) and into Freshwater East.
4. At the road junction and crossroads, go straight ahead along the B4584, signposted to Pembroke and Tenby. Follow the road as it sweeps round to the village of Lamphey.
5. At the staggered crossroad, rejoin the main road again (A4139) and head across the railway bridge.
6. At the T-junction beyond the church, where the main road takes a right-angle bend left, turn right to join the

Ridgeway, signposted to Tenby and Lamphey Palace. Almost immediately, turn left—near the sign to the Court Hotel, the magnificent building to be seen across the fields—and follow the lane, signposted to Lamphey Palace, to the ruins of the former bishops' 'holiday home'.

7. After exploring the ruins, return to the Ridgeway. Turn left and head towards Tenby—passing the Dial Inn as you leave Lamphey—and climb up onto the low hills of the Ridgeway proper, following signs to Tenby and Penally. Although not steep, this climb calls for sustained hard work. The Ridgeway is followed for about 4½ miles—ignoring all side turnings—in the direction of Manorbier. Take the fourth turn to the right (after leaving Lamphey) at a crossroads a short distance beyond the T-junction signposted to Manorbier railway station.

8. Follow the road down under the railway as far as the main A4139.

9. Go straight over the crossroads and head along the B4585. Follow the road through the village to the T-junction, signposted Manorbier Beach car park, where you turn left to regain the start of the route.

Carreg Coetan Arthur, Newport (Ride 8).

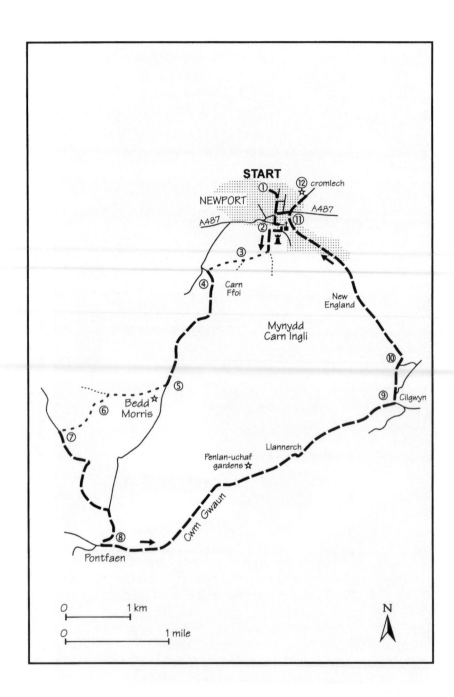

START
① ⑫ cromlech
NEWPORT
A487
A487
②
③
④ Carn
Ffoi
Mynydd
Carn Ingli
New
England
⑩
⑤
⑨ Cilgwyn
⑥ Bedd
Morris
⑦
Llannerch
Penlan-uchaf
gardens
Cwm Gwaun
⑧
Pontfaen

0   1 km

0   1 mile

N

8 Newport

Fact File

Distance:	12½ miles (20.1 km)
Time:	2-3 hours
Maps:	OS Landranger 145 Cardigan & Mynydd Preseli; OS Outdoor Leisure 35 North Pembrokeshire
Start:	Newport car park SN 057392
Nearest Towns:	Cardigan and Fishguard
Terrain:	Mainly on quiet lanes and tracks with one section on almost trackless moorland and fields. A long but fairly easy angled climb and a steep descent on lanes. Can be muddy in places.
Refreshments:	Newport: pubs, cafes and shops Cwm Gwaun: Dyffryn Arms ('Bessie's'), Pontfaen; Penlan-uchaf Gardens and tearoom
Parking:	See Start
Gates:	8—some in awful condition! One may be locked, but it is easy enough to lift your bike over the adjoining fence
Suitable for:	Family cycling. Good brakes are needed!
Cycle Hire:	Newport Mountain Bike Hire, Llysmeddyg Guest House, East Street, Newport Tel: 01239 820008

Along the way

To enjoy this ride at its most spectacular, I suggest you visit Newport in late summer when both the gorse and heather are in flower on the hills, giving the moorland a superb colour.

Newport, now a quiet coastal town, was once a hive of activity, with shipbuilding and the trading of sea-borne goods centred at Parrog on the shores of Newport Bay, as well as being the chief centre of the Barony of Cemais. The town itself is a Norman settlement and at its centre stands the much altered remains of a Norman castle (now a private house) and the nearby church with its sturdy Norman tower. Founded by Martin of Tours, Newport was given its charter some time before 1215 and the town still maintains its ancient rights and traditions. The ancient Court Lee meets regularly and the mayor, appointed by the Lady Marcher, is still called upon to perform ceremonies such as the Beating of the Bounds.

The area is rich in prehistoric remains, such as Carreg Coetan Arthur, a well-preserved Neolithic burial chamber to be found in Newport, and the Bronze Age standing stone of Bedd Morris on the slopes of Mynydd Caregog. Bedd Morris is wreathed in legend. Some say that the stone, now engraved as a parish boundary marker, marks the site of the hanging of a sheep stealer. It is claimed that Morris was an outlaw and highwayman who was eventually caught when a posse of outraged locals tracked his little white dog (trained to recover Morris' spent arrows) back to his hideout; both Morris and his dog supposedly lie buried in a pit beneath the stone. Others maintain that Morris was no outlaw but the loser in a duel for the love of the daughter of Pontfaen House. The restless romantic is still said to haunt the area around the stone. According to archaeologists, however, the stone was probably erected as a way marker during the second millenium BC. On a misty day, Bedd Morris and its surroundings certainly have an eerie atmosphere, but on a clear day provide superb views, especially eastwards in the direction of the Presely Hills.

Cwm Gwaun is a beautiful steep-sided valley flanked by ancient woodland, remote and individualistic with several sites of interest to visitors. The valley is noted for its wildlife and plants with rare lichens to be found (and left undamaged, please) at Sychpant Nature Reserve and Picnic Site, and for the historical oddity of keeping to the old Julian Calendar, long after the introduction of the Gregorian Calendar in 1582. Although this change had been adopted generally in Britain by 1752, it was ignored in Cwm Gwaun: Christmas and New Year are still celebrated here according to the Julian Calendar.

For those with a taste for tradition, a visit to what must be one of the most unspoilt rural pubs in Wales is recommended. The Dyffryn Arms, Pontfaen—better known as 'Bessie's', after the well-known landlady—serves excellent beer and is a must for any one fed up with plastic theme pubs and fake horse brasses.

The very sheltered Gwaun valley is also renowned for its gardens, especially those at Penlan-uchaf, which are open to the public throughout most of the year and delight the eye of any visitor.

The Candle Workshop and mini-museum of Cilgwyn Candles, near the bridge at Cilgwyn, is worth a visit. A wide selection of beautiful candles are for sale—many made on the premises—and the small, but intriguing museum outlines the history of candles and candle-making.

Mynydd Carn Ingli, whose rocky summit lies at the centre of this circular route, is crowned with a large Iron Age hill-fort. It was here that St Brynach came to commune with angels (see also ride 5), and some say that the summit rocks assume the figure of a reclining angel, lying on its back, wings spread beyond its head and hands clasped on its stomach, as it lies with its feet pointing north-east. If you visit the site, do take a compass and try and find the magnetic rock (said to have been Brynach's pillow) that can spin a compass needle right round. Held to be a 'place of power' by some modern pagans, Carn Ingli makes a noble backdrop to Newport and is just one of many interesting places to be visited on this ride.

Some of the place-names along the route are unusual, to say the least, and after completing the ride you will be able to boast of having cycled from Russia to New England in a matter of hours!

Route

1. From the entrance to the car park opposite the Pembrokeshire Coast National Park Information Centre (seasonal), turn right and head up the road, across the main A487 (take great care), towards the castle. At the top of Market Street, turn left and head along Church Street to visit the fine church. Continue a few yards along Church Street before turning right up Penffald.

2. This lane, below the castle, leads to a bridge by a ruined mill and a T-junction, where it joins Mill Lane. Turn left and follow Mill Lane steeply up-slope, past old settling tanks by a rushing stream and over a cattle grid to a junction of several tracks. Turn right and follow the track, identified with a bridleway fingerpost and signposted to Parc Glas Bach, Hill House and Fountain Hill.
3. Follow the track for about 500 yards, passing houses with superb views over Newport Bay, to a fork in the track. Take the right-hand fork past a ruined cottage and enjoy more views over the bay as you ride at the foot of the flank of Carn Ffoi, a rocky outcrop (said to be a sleeping giant) crowned by an Iron Age hill-fort. Continue along the track as far as the mountain road which heads over the hills.
4. Turn left and follow the road as it climbs at never too steep an angle up-slope and admire ever-expanding views as you gain height. On reaching the more level crest of the ridge, you will find Bedd Morris standing opposite the parking area.
5. Leave the road here and turn right into the field behind Bedd Morris. Follow the right-hand stone wall past the brick and concrete remains of some wartime military structures and on through two more rickety gates, as far as an obvious right-hand bend in the wall. Here, in an area littered with ancient cairns and hut circles, barely visible among the grass and rocks, bear left along a faint track heading just south of west to a gate in the fence on the far side of a stretch of often wet moor. Do not take the more obvious right-hand track.
6. Once through the gate and in the field, turn left, follow the fence for a short distance before swinging right along a barely discernible track which heads down to the south-west corner of the field, where you will find three gates. Leave the field through the right-hand gate (i.e. the gate furthest up-slope) and follow the left-hand fence to a gate which opens onto a surfaced lane. This section is due to be signposted and gated by the Pembrokeshire Coast National Park Authority, so the route should be easier to follow in the near future.

7. Turn left and follow the lane as it twists and turns (steeply, in places) down-slope, passing Russia and an intriguing turf-roofed cottage (where I have seen a goat grazing!), *en route* to a T-junction. Turn right, signposted to Cwm Gwaun, and follow the lane down a very steep hill with hairpin bends to the staggered crossroads at Pontfaen. Turn left, signposted to Penlan-uchaf Gardens, and head along the floor of the Gwaun valley.

8. Continue along the narrow, scenic road through Cwm Gwaun for about 3¾ miles. *En route* you will encounter the Dyffryn Arms (Bessie's); Sychbant Picnic Site with its nature trail, viewpoint, stream and well-maintained toilets; the entrance to Penlan-uchaf Gardens and tearooms (open from 9.00 till dusk); and Llannerch, where you may see a peacock and other fancy birds.

9. At the first T-junction beyond Llannerch, turn left and left again at the next T-junction, following signs to Newport and the Candle Workshop.

10. After visiting the Candle Workshop, continue up the steep lane near Cilgwyn Herb Garden and along Ffordd Cilgwyn, below the bulk of Carn Ingli. As you head towards Newport you will pass cottages called Plain Dealings and New England.

11. At the T-junction just beyond the 30 mph speed limit sign, on the outskirts of Newport, turn right and drop down to the A487 by the Acres Beach Art Gallery, which is well worth a visit. Turn left, then immediately right, down Pen y Bont, signposted to the Burial Chamber, Beach, Golf Club and Moylegrove. About 200 yards down the lane, turn left to enter a small estate of bungalows. Tucked away in the right-hand corner of the estate is Carreg Coetan Arthur, a 5,500 year old Neolithic burial chamber.

12. From the cromlech retrace your route back to the A487 and turn right. At the crossroads in the centre of Newport, turn right and return to the car park.

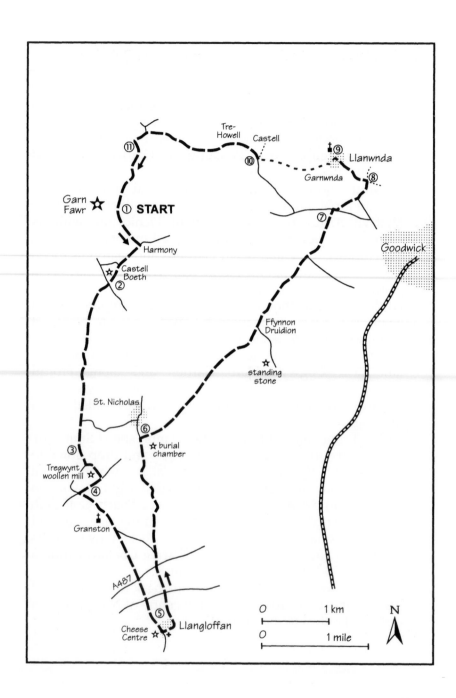

9 Around Garn Fawr and Llangloffan

Fact File

Distance:	13½ miles (21.7 km)
Time:	3 hours
Maps:	OS Landranger 157 St Davids & Haverfordwest; OS Pathfinder 1032 Fishguard; OS Outdoor Leisure 35 North Pembrokeshire
Start:	Garn Fawr car park SN 898388
Nearest Town:	Fishguard
Terrain:	Mainly on minor roads and lanes. The section along Feidr Pont Eglwys, beyond Llanwnda, can be muddy. There are some stiff climbs, notably at the end of the ride.
Refreshments:	Tearooms at Melin Tregwynt woollen mill and Llangloffan Cheese Centre.
Parking:	See Start
Gates:	1 (often open)
Suitable for:	Family cycling

Along the way

This cycle route takes in some superb scenery with beautiful views, especially from the summit of Garn Fawr. This ancient hill-fort, with its remains of Iron Age defences, as well as a wartime look-out, is one of many prehistoric sites which lie close to the route described. Other antiquities include Ffyst Samson (SN 907348) and Carnwnda (SN 933393); standing stones at SN 393390 and 921366; and another possible Iron Age fort, Castell Boeth, at SN 897377.

Llanwnda is the site of a holy well (situated just over the fence on the path to Carreg Wastad); and a beautiful Celtic-style double bellcote church which possibly stands on an ancient site. Ancient engraved stones are also found set into the church's exterior wall: four bear simple crosses and a fifth depicts a be-shawled face, perhaps of the Virgin Mary. Inside the church, a head is carved on one of the medieval beams.

Llanwnda Church (Ride 9)

Lancych Mansion (Ride 1)

The French, whose 1797 abortive invasion started at nearby Carreg Wastad, tried and failed to burn down this simple atmospheric church.

Melin Tregwynt Woollen Mill is a fascinating place to visit —and admission is free! Here you can watch the various stages involved in weaving woollen fabrics, enjoy a break in the tearooms and visit the shop stocked with woollen goods and other craft objects. For more details, phone 01348 891225.

Llangloffan Cheese Centre not only arranges guided tours designed to explain the traditional cheesemaking process, but also has a shop where you can buy a variety of excellent local cheeses, a tea shop/museum and a play area. Here you can meet the Jersey cows that make the milk that makes the cheese, as you wander around the farm. For more details, phone 01348 891241.

The quiet lanes followed on this ride are smothered in wild flowers in spring and early summer, while the variety of birdlife—both sea birds and inland species—is extraordinary.

Route

1. From the car park turn right and enjoy a free-wheel down to the T-junction at Harmony. Turn right, signposted to Pwllderi, Tremarchog/St Nicholas, and follow the road past a T-junction and Castell Boeth to a staggered crossroads.
2. The 'main' road swings left but our route heads straight across the crossroads and follows the lane signposted to Tregwynt Woollen Mill and Abermawr. You can now enjoy a mainly downhill run for 2 miles past Felindre and Tre Sisillt farms, until you come to a T-junction opposite some greenhouses at the bottom of a steep descent.
3. Turn left and follow the signpost to Tregwynt Woollen Mill, situated about 300 yards from the junction, a little way beyond an often dry watersplash. After enjoying a visit, continue along the lane to a T-junction about 200 yards beyond the mill.
4. Turn right and 400 yards further on, turn left at a crossroads and follow the lane—it climbs steeply at times—past

Granston Hall and a very attractively-sited church in the village of Granston. Beyond the village, bear right at the first junction and head straight on across two crossroads, following signs to Llangloffan Cheese Centre, a charming and informative gastronomes' delight.

5. A must for any cheese-lover, the centre provides another opportunity for rest and refreshment before you continue the short distance along the road to the T-junction opposite the Baptist chapel in Llangloffan. Turn left along the road signposted to Tremarchog/St Nicholas. You may enjoy excellent views as you follow this lane for about 2 miles, across two crossroads and down to a third, about 400 yards short of St Nicholas.

6. At the crossroads, turn right, signposted Wdig/Goodwick 3. On the high ground on your right is Ffyst Samson burial chamber which, along with other prehistoric relics, can be reached via the footpath (no cycling!) on your right, 400 yards from the crossroads. Continue along the lane for 3 miles, passing Ffynnon Druidion farm (turn right here to visit the nearby standing stone) and on to Henner Cross.

7. Go straight across the staggered crossroads at Henner Cross and along the narrow lane next to the telephone box, signposted Single Track Road. Bear left at the first T-junction and continue to the second T-junction, about half a mile beyond Henner Cross.

8. Turn left and follow the lane, signposted to Llanwnda, and head down to the green in front of the church.

9. Turn left and follow Feidr Pont Eglwys, a lane signposted Unsuitable For Motors, past Llanwnda house. Take the right fork and follow this often muddy 'white road' for some ¾ mile to a surfaced lane near the drive to Castell, a house built inside the banks of an ancient fort.

10. Do not go down to Castell, but turn right and follow the surfaced lane past Tre-Howel, where the French invasion force of 1797 signed their surrender, and on to a T-junction.

11. Turn left, signposted to Tremarchog/St Nicholas and Abermawr and Unsuitable For Coaches, and prepare yourself for a stiff climb back to the start. All those pleasant downhill free-wheeling rides are now to be paid for with effort!

Celtic cross in Nevern churchyard (Ride 5).

Old Manordeifi Church (Ride 2).

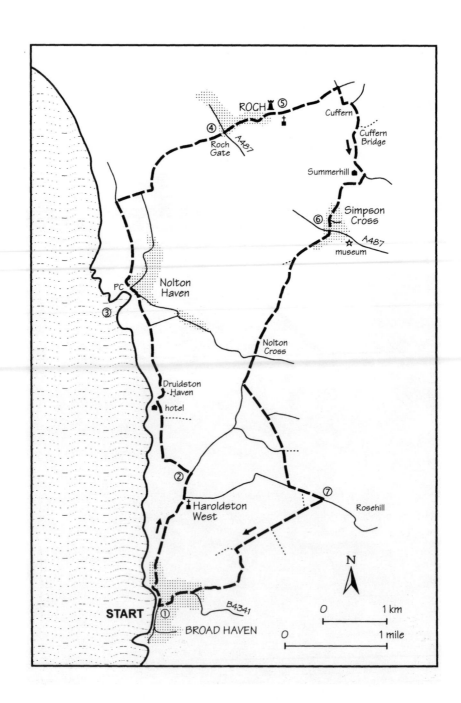

ROCH

Cuffern

⑤

Cuffern
Bridge

④

Roch
Gate

A487

Summerhill

Simpson
Cross

⑥

A487

museum

PC

Nolton
Haven

③

Nolton
Cross

Druidston
Haven

hotel

②

⑦

Haroldston
West

Rosehill

N

START

①

B4341

BROAD HAVEN

0   1 km

0   1 mile

58

10 Broad Haven and Roch

Fact File

Distance:	14 miles (22.5 km)
Time:	4-5 hours
Maps:	OS Landranger 157 St Davids & Haverfordwest; OS Pathfinder 1079 Haverfordwest; OS Pathfinder 1056 Newgale & Wolfscastle; OS Outdoor Leisure 36 South Pembrokeshire
Start:	T-junction on Broad Haven sea front SM 861138
Terrain:	Mainly traffic-free lanes; some steep climbs and descents on the coastal section.
Refreshments:	Broadhaven: pubs, cafes and shops Nolton Haven: The Mariners Inn Roch Gate: cafe and shop and Roch Gate Simpson Cross: tearooms and shop
Parking:	Broad Haven has ample parking provision, having two good car parks with toilets
Suitable for:	Those who enjoy 'roller-coaster' riding and pushing!
Cycle Hire:	Haven Sports, Marine Road, Broad Haven, Tel: 01437 781354.

Along the way

This ride takes you through some beautiful countryside and offers some superb views along the coast and out to sea, as well as of the Presely Hills.

Along the coastal section there is an opportunity to visit two beaches, Broad Haven and Nolton Haven, both of which will appeal to families and particularly children (of all ages, myself included!) with sand-castle building ambitions, while the cliffs between the two bays will reward you with some of the best views on the ride.

As you head out of Broad Haven up Haroldstone Hill, spare some breath to look for standing stones in the hedge by Upper Lodge. According to a 19th-century description these are

59

Manorbier Castle (Ride 7).

Cresswell Quay at high tide (Ride 3).

claimed to be the remains of a stone circle associated with Harold's Stone, which stands in the back garden of St Catherine's, a bungalow a little higher up the hill. The 5' 6" high stone is probably of Bronze Age origin and is one of three in Pembrokeshire bearing the name of Harold, who remains anonymous!

Druidstone Haven, despite its romantic name, appears not to have been named after any pre-Christian ceremonial stone, but recalls a Norman by the name of Drue who held land in the area. A disappointing origin to an intriguing place-name.

Nolton Haven is a steep-sided, narrow inlet and seems an appropriate place to be associated with piracy; it being said that local pirates once used this secluded, safe haven for their nefarious activities. More mundanely, this was once a coal-exporting beach. The remains of the old coal quay, built in 1769, can be made out, and it is interesting, and doubtless a little worrying to those committed to maintaining the 'unspoilt' character of the area, to learn that there are coal reserves left unmined in the area. If you look down seawards about ¾ mile north of Nolton, you can see the ruined chimney stack of Trefrân Cliff Colliery, which closed in 1905.

Although now metalled, the section of road between the old colliery and Druidstone Haven, which runs parallel to the Pembrokeshire Coast long-distance footpath, appears to have been part of one of the old pilgrim routes to St Davids Cathedral, a very important place of pilgrimage in the Middle Ages.

Inland, Roch Castle, on its volcanic outcrop, dominates the view. This 13th-century castle has a single, D-shaped tower, but would also once have boasted a ditched and banked bailey. Situated on the Landsker, the invisible boundary between the area colonised by the Normans—so-called 'little England beyond Wales'—and the Welshry, the domain of the native Welsh population, the castle was built by the Roche family, followers of Strongbow and who invaded Ireland with him in the 12th century.

Legend has it that Adam de la Roche was convinced he would die from being bitten by a snake, and so built the castle as a defence against all serpents. Unfortunately, a snake, brought in with a load of firewood, foiled the castle's defences and Adam's premonition came to pass! The castle was the birthplace of Lucy Walter, Charles II's mistress and mother of the unfortunate Duke of Monmouth. It is still a private residence, having been modernised in 1900, when a new wing was added, and is now available as a rather superior holiday let. Unfortunately, there is no public admittance, though the exterior is readily seen from the road.

The lovely church of St Mary's nestles in the shadow of the castle and, judging by its position inside a circular churchyard and other clues, it would appear to have Celtic origins. The present church is well-maintained with some interesting memorial plaques and stained-glass windows, including one featuring a Boy Scout in full uniform.

A short diversion east along the A487 from Simpson Cross brings you to the fascinating Motor Museum, which is well worth an extended visit even if, as a cyclist, you despise the lane-blocking, pollution-spewing modern car. Some of the vintage models are works of art.

This ride has plenty to interest the inquisitive cyclist and, despite the coastal climbs, is not too exhausting! Keep an eye open for the rich array of wild flowers and birds, from gulls to larks and buzzards, as well as signs of diverse mammal life.

Route

1. From Broad Haven sea front, head north along the coast road, signposted to Nolton and Newgale, climbing up Haroldstone Hill to Haroldstone West. At the T-junction by the pleasantly situated Church of St Madoc of Ferns, bear left (straight on), signposted to Nolton.
2. Some 400 yards further on is another T-junction where you turn left and follow a lane, signposted to Druidston Haven. This lane is crossed by cattle grids and, for part of its length, is only hedged on one side. It takes you steeply down a winding descent, past a hotel, then equally steeply up again the other side. At the next T-junction go straight on, following the lane to Nolton Haven.

Colliery remains, Nolton Haven (Ride 10).

At the junction beyond the United Reformed Church, whose south-facing wall displays some fascinating patterns of erosion, turn left and descend to the beach, past an old spring built into the wall below the church and near the Mariners Inn.

3. You are now faced by the last really steep climb of the ride, which leads you up past old colliery workings on your left to a T-junction about 1 mile from Nolton Haven. A short distance past Cliff Cottage, which overlooks the ruins of Trefrân Cliff Colliery, turn right.

4. This zigzag lane rises, dips and rises again as it approaches Roch. At the crossroads at Roch Gate, go straight across the A487 and head for the castle.

5. Follow the lane past the castle and church, ignoring residential side turns, to a crossroads. Turn right, signposted to Cuffern, and at the next T-junction turn right again down to Cuffern Bridge, near the delightfully named dingle of Frogs Hole.

   At the next T-junction, by Summerhill farm, bear right and follow the wider lane, which brings you into Simpson Cross on the A487.

6. Taking great care, go straight over the crossroads and down the lane opposite, signposted to Nolton Cross Caravan Park. Follow the lane to Nolton Cross. At the crossroads, head straight on along the lane signposted to Broad Haven. At the T-junction about 450 yards ahead, turn left, signposted to Haverfordwest. Follow the lane—ignoring the road entering from the left—over a crossroads to yet another T-junction. Bear left and follow the minor road, signposted to Haverfordwest.

7. Some 500 yards ahead turn sharp right, almost doubling back on yourself at an unsigned T-junction, into Long Lane, which heads in a dead straight line for 1¼ miles, then wiggles its way down to the outskirts of Broad Haven. At the T-junction at the end of Long Lane, turn right to sweep down to the sea front and regain the start of the ride.

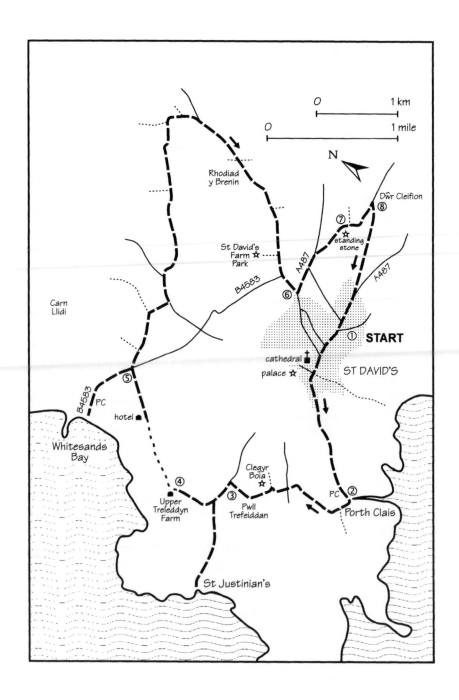

11 St Davids

Fact File

Distance: 9½ miles (15.2 km) to 12½ miles (20.1 km), depending on options taken

Time: 2-3 hours; add extra for visits to places *en route*

Maps: OS Landranger 157 St Davids & Haverfordwest; OS Outdoor Leisure 35 North Pembrokeshire

Start: Car park near the Pembrokeshire Coast National Park visitor centre SN 757252

Nearest Town: St Davids

Terrain: Mainly easy cycling on quiet lanes, but one short, steep climb; two sections on the A487; one potentially very muddy section.

Refreshments: St Davids: shops, pubs, cafes
Whitesands Bay: shop (seasonal)
Ice cream vans may be parked at Whitesands Bay, Porth Clais and St Justinian's, in season

Parking: See Start

Suitable for: Family cycling

Cycle Hire: Coastal Trader Booking Office, High Street, St Davids Tel: 01437 721611

Along the way

Although only short, this ride takes in some wonderful scenery and passes sites of great interest. St Davids itself, the smallest city in Britain, is of course the most obvious attraction, with its famous cathedral and Bishop's Palace.

The present cathedral, situated on the floor of Glyn Rhosyn, a sheltered valley, was started by Bishop Peter de Leia in 1181 on the site of an earlier Christian settlement but was not completed until the early 16th century. It is well worth an extended visit: look out for the 'green men' carvings, pre-Christian symbols incorporated into the decoration, showing a certain amount of hedging of spiritual bets on the part of the Christian builders.

Legends offer two quite different explanations for the cathedral being half-hidden in a valley. One is that the pagan rulers of the land only granted the first Christian settlers the worst, boggy, disease-ridden marshy ground in the area for building their church and homes, in the hope that they would either succumb to disease and die, or be so discouraged as to leave for a more attractive site. Alternatively, it has been suggested that the early Christians hid in the valley to avoid the attentions of pagan sea raiders, who might have endangered the life of the community and looted the church. Whatever the reason, St Davids cathedral sits snugly in its secluded site and now attracts tourists, as it once attracted pilgrims. At one time St Davids was a renowned and important place of pilgrimage, for it was Pope Calixtus the second who decreed that two pilgrimages to St Davids was equal to one to Rome itself. St Davids was also the seat of the most powerful bishops in Wales.

The Bishop's Palace, built between 1328 and 1347 by Bishop Gower, is now, sadly, a ruin but was probably the most splendid in Britain. The crumbled remains, a calm and relaxing place to visit after a ride, show how vainglory, in the form of an earthly paradise, does not always stand the test of time.

Legend also tells of how Porth Clais harbour, which served St Davids, was the site where Twrch Trwyth, a great black boar, swam ashore from Ireland and was pursued across Pembrokeshire and the Presely Hills by King Arthur and his knights. The tale is vividly recalled in *The Mabinogion*. Porth Clais was, until the early years of the 20th century, an important harbour. The old limekilns, within which limestone was burned to produce lime for sweetening the acid soils of the area, have been restored by the National Trust but no mention is made of the gasworks, which is now a car park.

On being excavated by archaeologists, Clegyr Boia, whose rocky ramparts are made of very ancient volcanic ash, proved to have been occupied from Neolithic times to around the 6th century, when the legendary chieftain Boia, after whom the site is named, was converted from his pagan, pirate ways by Christians who had settled in Glyn Rhosyn. It then appears that Boia used his power and influence to protect the religious settlement from neighbouring pagans and his piratical friends, until he himself was killed by a pirate. Boia, however, was given a Christian burial by St David, the patron saint of Wales. High on the steep western side of Clegyr Boia there is a tiny well said to have the power to cure eye ailments. But the well, although said never to dry up in a drought or to overflow its rim, is difficult to find, for it is only the size of your cupped hands and holds about half a pint of water.

A 'there and back' optional diversion takes you off the main route to St Justinian's, where it is possible to see the ruins of a chapel on the site of a Celtic oratory, as well as a striking lifeboat house and slipway that featured in a BBC series called . . . 'Lifeboat'!

The main route takes you to Whitesands Bay, terminus of two Roman roads and a supposed ancient gold trading route from southern England and beyond. The bay, though now more famous for its sand and surf, was also the site of a chapel dedicated to St Patrick, the patron saint of Ireland.

The slopes of Carn Llidi, the steep and rocky hill above the northern end of the beach, are littered with the remains of Neolithic burial chambers, and on its summit are the remains of a Second World War hydrophone and radar station. Between Carn Llidi and St Davids Head, lies Coetan Arthur, a fine Neolithic burial chamber, and traces of Iron Age settlements and field systems. Carn Llidi along with Carn Penbiri, about 2 miles to the north-west, looms over the whole of the St Davids peninsula, dotted with rocky outcrops and boggy hollows.

At Rhodiad y Brenin the route crosses the line of Ffos y Mynach, the Monk's Dyke, said to be an ancient ditch and bank marking the boundary of church lands. Monks were not allowed beyond the boundary, but within its bounds special rights of sanctuary existed. Ffos y Mynach is encountered again near Dŵr Cleifion (Water of the Sick) where it is said the sick would seek healing.

The scenery *en route* is varied and the flora and fauna—in season—quite breathtaking. The sea is the domain of seals, dolphins and sea birds galore, whilst in spring and early summer the hedges and fields along the way are ablaze with wildflowers in bloom.

The rare breeds survival centre at St Davids Farm Park and the award-winning Marine Life Centre in St Davids are both worthy of extended visits.

Route

1. From the car park by the visitor centre rejoin the main road, turn left and ride into the centre of this mini city. At the old Market Cross and war memorial garden, which occupy a triangular patch of ground, turn left, signposted to Porth Clais and St Justinian's. Ignoring side turns, follow the zigzag road along the rim of Glyn Rhosyn (Merry Vale) (on the banks of the river Alun is an old mill complete with leat and wheel) which leads steeply down to Porth Clais. Note the stone slab footbridge over the river Alun.

2. Unfortunately, the steep descent is matched by a steep but short climb out of the narrow valley, but you are soon on more level ground. At the crossroads, approximately half a mile beyond Porth Clais, go straight ahead, signposted to St Justinian's, and follow the lane between the craggy ramparts of Clegyr Boia and the marshy Pwll Trefeiddan to a T-junction.

3. Turn left at the junction, signposted to St Justinian's, and continue to a fork in the road some 300 yards ahead. Here you have the choice of *either* following the 'main' road to St Justinian's before retracing your route back to the fork, *or* the main route which forks right, signposted as a dead end.

4. Do not be put off cycling along this trackway for, despite being waymarked as a footpath (there is no right to cycle on footpaths), it is actuallly a bridleway (indicated by the smaller, blue arrows) on which you can walk, ride a horse or bicycle. It is hoped that the route will be waymarked accurately in the near future.

Where the surfaced lane swings left at Upper Treleddyn farm, head straight on through the farmyard and follow the track as it swings right. The track is initially a grassy green lane (often very muddy in wet weather) before becoming a more solid trackway which regains its surface near the Whitesands Bay Hotel. At the end of the lane leading to the hotel is a staggered crossroads.

5. You can *either* turn left and take the B4583 to Whitesands Bay before returning to the crossroads, *or* go straight on, and follow the main route up the lane opposite, signposted to the Youth Hostel. Follow the lane for a little over half a mile, past the turn to the Youth Hostel and a caravan park (the museum marked on some OS maps no longer exists), to a T-junction where you turn left. Continue for approximately 1¾ miles, ignoring turns to the left, until you come to a T-junction that you approach on the minor road. Turn right and head back towards St Davids, passing through the hamlet of Rhodiad y Brenin (the King's Causeway), which was probably on one of the old pilgrim routes to St Davids.

6. This quiet road, followed for about 1½ miles, joins the B4583 from Whitesands Bay at a T-junction. At the next T-junction, where the B4583 joins the A487 by the St Davids Rugby Club, turn left (take great care). Follow the fairly busy road for approximately 450 yards to the second lane on the right (not the one leading to a factory). After turning up this quiet lane, note the large standing stone on your right as you swing south towards Trecenny farm.

7. Some 250 yards beyond the farm, you come to a T-junction by Dŵr Cleifion, where the waters often flood over the road (there's a pedestrian bridge beside the road).

8. At the junction, before the stream, turn sharp right and continue as far as the T-junction where you rejoin the A487. Turn right at the junction and head past the school and Marine Life Centre, to reach the car park, the starting point of the ride.

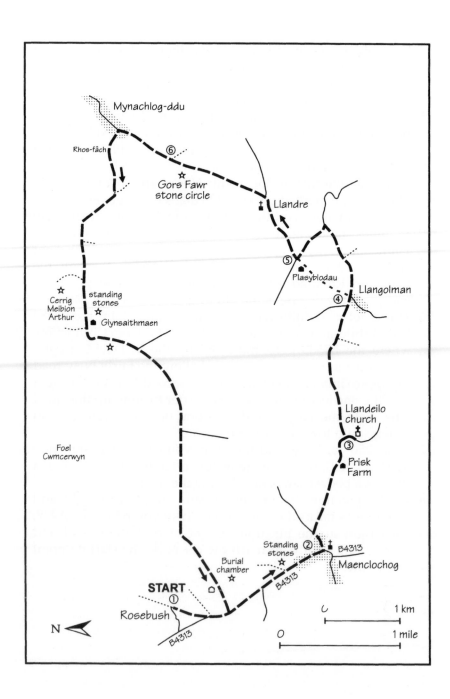

12 Rosebush and Gors Fawr

Fact File

Distance:	13 miles (20.9 km) or 12½ miles (20.1 km)
Time:	3-4 hours
Maps:	OS Landranger 145 Cardigan & Mynydd Preseli; OS Pathfinder 1057 Ambleston and Llandissilio; OS Outdoor Leisure 35 North Pembrokeshire
Start:	The Old Post Office, Rosebush SN 074294
Nearest Town:	Fishguard
Terrain:	Mainly (or all, if no diversion is taken) on country lanes. Several short, sharp climbs, but mainly gently rolling country lanes. In places the lanes may flood to become fords.
Refreshments:	Rosebush: Tafarn Sinc Presely pub, shop and the Old Post Office tearooms, restaurant and bistro Maenclochog: The Globe Inn and shops
Parking:	Near the Old Post Office, Rosebush
Gates:	2
Suitable for:	Family cycling

Along the way

The small village of Rosebush owes its existence to the now disused slate quarries that used to produce slabs and roofing slate. Since the quarries closed early in the 20th century, the old workings have mellowed with age but remain a site of great interest to industrial archaeologists. During the latter part of the 19th century and the early years of the 20th century the railway, originally opened to serve the quarrying industry, was advertised as a tourist attraction, bringing visitors to admire the wildness of the Presely Hills. Tafarn Sinc Presely, formerly the Prescelly Hotel, was built to receive these visitors. Sadly, it no longer offers accommodation within its locally famous corrugated-iron walls, but serves as a pub noted for its warm Welsh atmosphere. Within the garden is a re-creation of a railway halt.

The Maenclochog railway was built by Edward Cooper (1799-1877) and memorials to his memory are to be found on private land near the remains of Rosebush station and inside Maenclochog Church. The church, dedicated to St Mary, is set in the centre of Maenclochog village and is on an ancient site, the original wooden church, some say, having being burned by the Irish marauders. It is now in good condition and is served by a very keen vicar, Michael Grainger, but this has not always been the case. One early vicar, a certain William Crowther, was upbraided in 1743 for immoral behaviour, negligence and drunkenness, including keeping a female housekeeper who had some 'base born' children (by him?), being too drunk to perform a wedding, and in labouring on the Sabbath!

The ruined church of St Teilo, a short distance off the main route, was once famous for its grisly relic of the saint—his skull, which is now kept in Llandaff cathedral. St Teilo was a 5th-century saint and friend of St David and St Padarn. As well as founding churches in Wales and Brittany (where he is the patron saint of horses and apples), St Teilo made a pilgrimage to Jerusalem where he was acclaimed for his humility and being even more Christ-like than his two companions, David and Padarn. Retiring to Carmarthenshire, St Teilo eventually died and produced not one, but three corpses so that he could be buried in each of three places wanting that privilege—Llandeilo Fawr (Carmarthen), Penally and Llandaff.

In the 15th century, Sir David Mathews restored the saint's tomb in Llandaff and was given the skull of St Teilo, set in a reliquary of some value, as a reward. The skull was held by the Mathews and Melchior families, becoming a drinking cup for use at the holy well near St Teilo's church, Llandeilo, whose waters effected a cure for whooping cough. The skull eventually found its way, via Winchester, to Australia when the Mathews family—and the family heirloom—moved. In 1994, the skull was returned to Llandaff cathedral (founded by St Teilo) by Captain Mathews, the last hereditary 'guardian of the skull', where it can be seen in its beautiful mounting.

However, tests carried out on the skull in 1927 indicate that the 'relic' is of 14th- or 15th-century date, not 6th century. A well-researched booklet *The Legend of St Teilo's Skull* by Anthony Bailey, is available from the newsagents in Maenclochog, the village where many of Llandeilo's treasures now reside. Two of the three ancient, inscribed stones, formerly associated with St Teilo's church, Llandeilo, are to be found in St Mary's, Maenclochog. They stand inside the church, near the door: one reads '(the stone) of Curcagnus, son of Cavetus. He lies (here)', and the other '(the stone) of Coimagnus, son of Andagellus, son of Cavetus'. The third stands in the graveyard of Cenarth church, on the banks of the river Teifi, and the inscription reads '(the stone) of Curcagnus, son of Andagellus'. The stones now in St Mary's church were moved in 1959 to help preserve them from the weather.

The third church visited *en route* is the church of St Dogmaels at Llandre, near Mynachlog-ddu. This is again on an ancient site and, like St Mary's, Maenclochog, was at one time an outlier of St Dogmaels Abbey near Cardigan. Unfortunately, unlike St Mary's, this church has to be kept locked, but it is a very pleasant, double-aisled building, the northern aisle being 16th century and the nave Victorian in date. Today it is looked after by the Reverend Michael Grainger.

Ancient sites abound on this ride. On the approach to Maenclochog from Rosebush, two standing stones are visible from the lane on the left-hand side of the road near the 30 mph limit signs, some 600 yards short of St Mary's church, while a rocky mound to the south of the church is said to be an ancient castle site. Another stone stands in the field on your right just beyond Prisk Farm (SN 097271) and opposite Druidstone House, a Georgian facaded house originally designed by John Nash, while at Gors Fawr, near Mynachlog-ddu, there is a well-known Bronze Age stone circle with two attendant standing stones set in the middle of open moorland.

At Rhos-fach, Mynachlog-ddu, is a recent standing stone erected to commemorate Waldo Williams (1904-71), one of Wales' best loved poets of recent times, and staunch pacifist. The memorial plaque is inscribed with a couplet from one of his best known poems, 'Preseli'. Nearby, on the opposite side of the road which crosses Rhos-fach, stands another recent 'bluestone' monument, commemorating the transport of bluestones from the vicinity of Carn Meini to Stonehenge in both ancient and more modern times, and erected as a celebration of the Cystic Fibrosis Trust's Silver Jubilee in 1989.

On the ride back to Rosebush you will pass at least four more standing stones, an ancient homestead and the remains of a burial chamber, all close to the road. The first pair of stones, Cerrig Meibion Arthur, said to be Arthur's sons turned to stone during their attempt to catch Twrch Trwyth, the great black boar, are best seen looking north-east from the bridge over Afon Wern near Glynsaithmaen. They stand approximately 400 yards away but are often hard to make out. Looking south-west from the same spot another standing stone can be seen close to the field boundary. Although only some 200 yards away, this stone is also difficult to see unless you get very close. A fourth standing stone may be seen in the field on your right about 300 yards beyond a 90° left-hand bend in the lane. The ancient settlement and burial chamber are more easily seen (using some imagination, as both are only traces), on your left, opposite Mount Pleasant, a ruined farm, some 500 yards or so from the T-junction, where the minor road from Glynsaithmaen meets the B4313.

The summit of Foel Cwmcerwyn is the highest point in south-west Wales and, as well as having a topping of Bronze Age cairns, overlooks the prehistoric 'Gold road' that supposedly ran along the ridge of the Presely Hills, linking the Salisbury Plain area of southern England to Whitesands Bay, the point where Irish gold traders came ashore. The east-face of Foel Cwmcerwyn is scarred by slate mining, as are the slopes above Rosebush.

Some of the lanes used on this ride have historical connections with the old drovers' routes. Indeed, Maenclochog was once an important droving centre, as well as being a railway centre located on the Fishguard and Maenclochog railway.

In all, this ride takes you from the present, through the Victorian era, into the prehistoric past, and in so doing encompasses Arthurian and Celtic myths and legends while passing through some superb countryside. Panoramic views and wildlife abound: look out in particular for buzzards and ravens.

Route

1. From the car park, return to the lane leading to the old Post Office, turn right and head for the junction with the B4313, ignoring the turn down to Tafarn Sinc. Turn left, and follow this quiet road for a little over half a mile into the centre of Maenclochog.
2. Almost opposite St Mary's Church, turn left between the shop and the garage, signposted to Mynachlog-ddu and Crymych. At a T-junction, 150 yards beyond a bridge over a stream, turn right, signposted to Llangolman and ride down past Prisk Farm to another T-junction. Here you can *either* turn right, signposted to Llanycefn, to visit the ruins of Llandeilo Church, *or* continue straight on.
3. If you choose to visit the church, follow the right-hand fork for some 150 yards to a farm. Leave your bike and walk through the gateway between the barns, follow a track by the end of the house and through a gate; turn right at the wall to enter the ruinous churchyard via a rickety gate. After visiting the ruins, rejoin the main route, turning right along the lane and following the signs to Llangolman, ignoring all side turns. The lane is a winding switchback as it dips and climbs its way into and out of small valleys. It is quite tiring to ride but interesting, for deeply sunken sections flanked by high flower-covered banks and shaded by trees, alternate with open stretches providing good views. Footbridges for pedestrian use when the streams are in flood are found at the bottom of some of the dips.
4. At Llangolman, you have a choice of routes. Where a road joins from the right, a little way beyond the phone box, a bridle-way track goes left, signposted Plas-cwrt. Mainly quite well surfaced, this bridleway takes you across Llangolman Common via Plasyblodau farm, cutting out a mile of road cycling that includes a longish descent and complementary climb. However, between Plas-cwrt and

77

Plasyblodau you must fight your way for some 200 yards through—not over—what is possibly the roughest, boggiest track I have ever encountered while cycling. Those who do not carry their bikes will certainly have to push them!

Those who prefer road cycling can continue straight through the village, following the signs for Efailwen. At the first T-junction you encounter, turn left, signposted to Maenclochog, and climb half a mile to a second T-junction.

5. At the junction, turn right—joining the rough riders who rejoin the metalled road at this point—and head down the road signposted Unsuitable for Wide Vehicles, and to Mynachlog-ddu and Crymych. The road leads down to a narrow bridge which takes you over Afon Wern to a T-junction by St Dogmaels church. Turn left, signposted to Crymych, and follow the road for about ¾ mile to where a gate and kissing gate allow access to Gors Fawr and the stone circle. The circle is signposted at the gates.

6. After exploring this fascinating site, continue along the road for another ¾ mile. On reaching Mynachlogddu, turn left at a T-junction opposite a house on the right. Follow the narrow road, signposted to Rosebush, for the next 5 miles. The road skirts the Presely Hills, rising to your right, and heads past the Waldo memorial on Rhos-fach and Cerrig Meibion Arthur, near Glynsaithmaen, before joining the B4313 at a T-junction between Maenclochog and Rosebush. Turn right, signposted to Fishguard, then right again to enter Rosebush, the start of your ride.

Standing stones, Gors Fawr, Mynachlog-ddu (Ride 12).

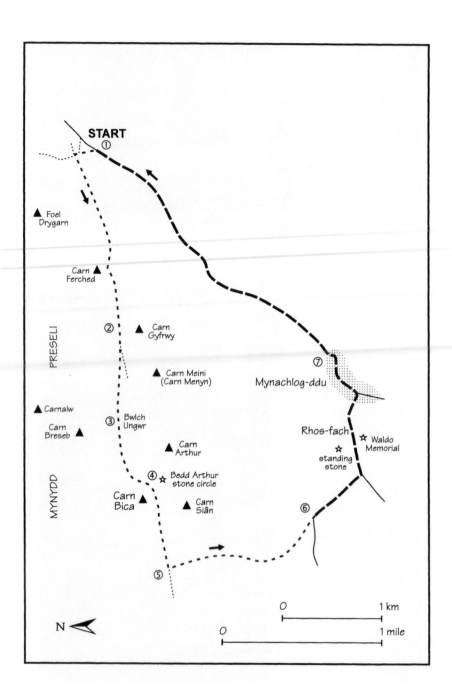

START ①

▲ Foel
Drygarn

Carn ▲
Ferched

PRESELI

② ▲ Carn
Gyfrwy

▲ Carn Meini
(Carn Menyn)

⑦

Mynachlog-ddu

▲ Carnalw

Carn ▲
Breseb

③ Bwlch
Ungwr

Rhos-fach

☆ Waldo
Memorial

▲ Carn
Arthur

☆ standing
stone

④ ☆ Bedd Arthur
stone circle

Carn ▲
Bica

▲ Carn
Siân

MYNYDD

⑥

⑤

N ◀

0   1 km

0   1 mile

13 The Golden Road and Rhos-fach

Fact File

Distance:	7 miles (11.2 km)
Time:	2-2½ hours
Maps:	OS Landranger 145 Cardigan & Mynydd Preseli; OS Pathfinder 1033 Newport (Trefdraeth) & Eglwyswrw; OS Outdoor Leisure 35 North Pembrokeshire
Start:	Roadside parking at SN165330
Terrain:	Hill tracks and quiet lanes. The hills can be very wet and muddy. To avoid excessive erosion, please do this ride only in dry weather, when your tyres will do less damage.
Refreshments:	None
Parking:	See Start
Gates:	1
Suitable for:	Mountain biking for the fit

PLEASE NOTE

Prevent Skids—ride with control to prevent erosion, especially in wet conditions.

Stay on the Trail—do not ride off the trail.

Be Courteous and Considerate—always give way to walkers and riders even if it means dismounting.

Be Safe: take Food, Whistle and Compass; wear a Helmet and carry Waterproofs and Spare Clothing—weather conditions on the Presely Hills can be very changeable.

Livestock—do not startle or disturb livestock, and respect the life of the countryside.

Along the way

Half of this route is on the open hill and half on quiet lanes. Many sites of prehistoric and historic interest lie along its 7 short miles.

Bedd Arthur, with Carn Menyn and Foel Drygarn (Ride 13).

Carreg Samson, Abercastle (Ride 14).

The first 3 miles can prove quite hard work as you climb on hill tracks, but the views make it all worthwhile. As some of the hill tracks are quite soft, and very soft in wet weather, I advise anyone contemplating this ride to undertake it during the summer when drier weather will prevent too much environmental damage being caused by tyres.

The first track you follow, leads along the crest of the mountain ridge and is part of the Golden Road or Fleming Way, a possible ancient trading route which led from Whitesands Bay, near St Davids, to southern England and beyond. This route was reputedly used to transport Irish gold in prehistoric times, and later by drovers and other long-distance travellers before the present-day road network was developed.

As you might expect, this ancient route is littered with historic monuments and traces of man's passing. The first and most obvious remains are the three Bronze Age cairns and Iron Age hill-fort on the summit of Foel Drygarn, the hill dominating the western end of this ride. With its many traces of hut circles and still very visible defensive walls, this fort must have been of great importance and, for those interested in such phenomena, appears to be sited at the junction of several ley lines.

Where the track levels out alongside the forest boundary, you pass by the remains of Carn Ferched, now a barely visible collection of stones, but once, it seems, a notable cairn. The track then climbs again, skirting an area of rock outcrops similar in appearance to the tors of Dartmoor. The most westerly of the outcrops is Carn Meini (Menyn), a fascinating jumble of joint-riven igneous rock from where some of the so-called bluestones of Stonehenge have originated.

To the north of these outcrops, on the lower slopes of the Presely Hills, is Carnalw, another Iron Age fort, which possesses clear and very elaborate defences that seem to be too grandoise for such a small site. These defences include a *cheveux de frise* (stones laid on edge to stop galloping horses and running men) and a well-defined and walled entrance. Carnalw's most recent brush with war was as a 'stand-in' for Tumbledown Mountain during the preparation of a BBC film about the Falklands War. Various bits of detritus, such as fired blank rounds of ammunition, can still be found amongst the ancient rocks.

A short distance west of Carn Meini is Bedd Arthur (Arthur's Grave), a very small stone circle, and Carn Bica with its Bronze Age cairns. Bedd Arthur is more of an ellipse than a circle and may indeed be the remains of an important grave, though some claim it is a solar or lunar observatory or calendar. Carn Bica, the last high point on this route, has had its cairns remodelled to form a couple of hollow wind shelters. I understand this was accomplished during the Second World War by members of the Home Guard who were here on guard duty during some of the many military manoeuvres that took place on these hills prior to the Normandy invasion.

The summit of Foel Cwmcerwyn occasionally witnesses religious ceremonies held by contemporary pagans, whilst the very steep, east-facing slopes below the summit once sheltered Pembrokeshire's last glacier. On the main ridge between Foel Cwmcerwyn and Carn Bica are Cerrig y Marchogion, rock outcrops which recall Arthur's knights involved in the furious hunt for Twrch Trwyth (for further details see also page 76).

On the downhill ride to the road at the foot of Talfynydd, you may enjoy a panoramic view over the middle reaches of the Cleddau Ddu and its tributaries. Above you on your left, halfway down the track, are the remains of a crashed Second World War bomber.

Between Talfynydd and Mynachlog-ddu is Rhos-fach with its monument to the Welsh poet, Waldo Williams, educated in Mynachlog-ddu junior school (now closed) and inspired by the area and its people (for further details see also page 75).

South of Rhos-fach is the small stone circle of Gors Fawr, with its attendant standing stones, said to be a celestial observatory or calendar.

On your return from Mynachlog-ddu the road follows the upper reaches of the Cleddau Ddu, a valley also containing, though less easily seen, standing stones and a prehistoric burial chamber.

This short ride takes in some wonderful scenery and fascinating sites and would make an excellent summer evening trip. Keep your eyes open for a variety of birds, from larks to buzzards, and a host of wild flowers in the valley.

Route

1. From the roadside parking area follow the track, signposted as a bridle path (a Pembrokeshire Coast National Park sign also declares 'No vehicles beyond this point'), up to the gate, beyond which lies the open hill. Go through the gate, turn left and follow the track up-slope, past the coniferous plantation on your left.
2. At Carn Gyfrwy, the first major rock outcrop on your left, (there is a small sheepfold at its foot) the track becomes more faint, and forks. Take the right-hand fork and head down-slope into Bwlch Ungwr.
3. On the floor of Bwlch Ungwr, about 2 miles from the start, the main track can be boggy in places. To avoid these peaty sections, take a loop right towards the rocky outcrops, where a fainter path skirts the fragile boggy sections. Rejoin the main track further on.
4. On approaching Carn Bica, the track again becomes faint and many branches are encountered. Take the most obvious path which zigzags up past Bedd Arthur and Carn Bica. Here the path becomes more obvious as it crosses the broad, peaty and often wet summit.
5. Beyond Carn Bica the route descends to the floor of a boggy saddle, where the ridge path is crossed by a faint north-south track. Turn left, just before you come to the worst of the bog, and follow the track southwards. Though wet and boggy in places, this path improves as you descend and in summer is a superb free-wheel ride.
6. All too soon, the track joins the tarmac road linking Rosebush and Mynachlog-ddu. Bear left (visually straight-on) and follow the road across Rhos-fach to Mynachlog-ddu.
7. At the T-junction, turn left, signposted to Crymych and Taith Preseli Tour, and follow this quiet road, bordered with trees and flower bedecked banks, to the start of the ride.

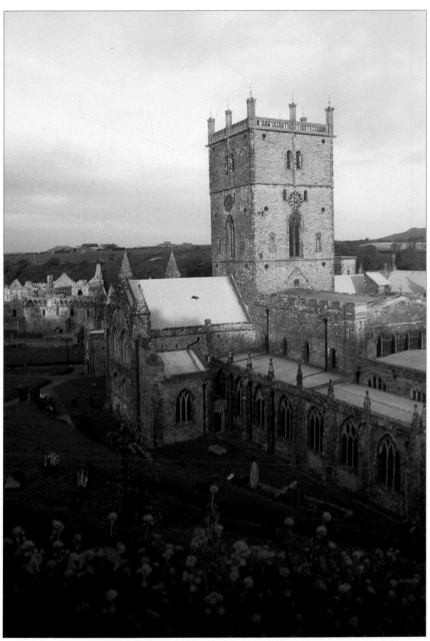

St Davids Cathedral and Bishop's Palace (Ride 11).

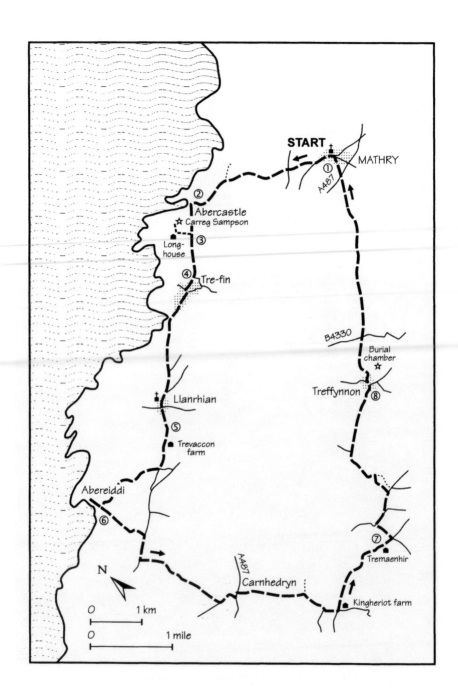

START

MATHRY

①

A487

②

Abercastle

☆ Carreg Sampson

Long-
house

③

④ Tre-fin

B4330

Burial
chamber

☆

Treffynnon ⑧

Llanrhian

⑤

• Trevaccon
farm

Abereiddi

⑥

⑦

Tremaenhir

N

A487

Carnhedryn

• Kingheriot farm

0   1 km

0   1 mile

14 Mathry

Fact File

Distance:	18 miles (28.9 km)
Time:	4 hours
Maps:	OS Landranger 157 St Davids & Haverfordwest; OS Outdoor Leisure 35 North Pembrokeshire
Start:	Mathry SM 878319
Nearest Town:	Fishguard and St Davids
Terrain:	Mostly quiet country lanes. Some short, sharp climbs, but mainly rolling countryside.
Refreshments:	Mathry: Farmers Arms
Trefin: Ship Inn and shop
Abereiddi: Trevaccoon Farm (seasonal cream teas) and ice cream van (seasonal)
Parking:	See Start. Limited parking by church and toilets
Suitable for:	Older children and anyone interested in history

Along the way

Along this route you will not only have an opportunity to follow a maze of narrow, quiet, winding lanes flanked by high hedge banks, but also to visit sites which prove that man has occupied this beautiful part of the county for a long, long time.

The described route starts at Mathry, a hill-top village that dominates the surrounding area. Central to the village is the Church of the Holy Martyrs, reminiscent of churches in France, as it has neither steeple nor tower. The present church, rebuilt in 1869, is the fifth place of worship known to have graced this site, the steeples of previous buildings acting as navigation markers for ships. Built into the west wall of the churchyard, are two early Christian stones bearing inscribed crosses within circles. One had previously been used as a gatepost. Inside the porch is another 5th- or 6th-century stone with a Latin inscription that translates as 'Maccudiccl, son (of) Caticuus, (lies here)'. On the back of the stone is an Ogam inscription of uncertain meaning.

The Blue Lagoon, Abereiddy (Ride 14).

Remains of Narberth castle (Ride 6).

On the coast, north-west of Mathry, is the tiny settlement of Abercastle, a narrow and well-protected natural harbour. Above the hamlet is the imposing and well-preserved Neolithic burial chamber, Carreg Sampson. From here you can enjoy superb views: the vista north-eastwards over the sea to Pen-caer (which also boasts some fine *cromlechi*) is particularly impressive. The community who built Carreg Sampson certainly had an eye for a good view.

Tre-fin, a little further down the coast, is a charming village, and home to a hand-weaving centre. It was the birthplace of Edgar Phillips, a former archdruid of Wales who adopted Tre-fin as his bardic name. Melin Tre-fin, the ruined corn mill at nearby Aberfelin, also inspired another archdruid—Crwys (William Crwys Williams) to write one of his finest lyric poems.

South-west of Tre-fin and Abereiddi, Carn Penbiri, a craggy hill, dominates the view: although not visited, it looms over the surrounding countryside. Much of the remains of a prehistoric settlement on its slopes have been quarried away.

Abereiddi is a fascinating spot and was once the scene of intense industrial activity, the cliffs on the north side of the beach being quarried for slate. After the quarry was closed in 1904, the seaward side of the workings was blown up to create what is now known as the Blue Lagoon, a safe haven for small boats. This is now a favourite spot for diving, coasteering and pleasure boats. The ruined cottages at the north end of the beach were destroyed in the great storm of 1938, while disease —a typhoid epidemic in the 1920s—also played its part in the abandonment of the street. The circular building on the headland is said to have been where the quarry manager's wife entertained other ladies to tea and where board meetings were held. It also formed a day mark for ships navigating the coast. The dark grey shales exposed in the centre of the bay are noted for their graptolite fossils, the remains of creatures which thrived in the sea some 470 million years ago. Please do not damage or remove any fossils you discover.

Inland, north-east of Solva more relics of the past are found: two impressive standing stones at Tremaenhir, and in a field to the east of Treffynon there is another burial chamber.

Although this corner of Pembrokeshire witnessed much

industrial activity in the past, it is now largely the province of farmers and tourists. The area is also noted for its wonderful display of wild flowers in spring and early summer, while overhead there is a great diversity of bird life, particularly sea birds and peregrine falcons along the coastal section.

Route

1. From Mathry, pass by the west end of the church and take the road signposted to Abercastle, which heads in a north-westerly direction past the Mathry Community Hall. At the fork in the road, where you will encounter the first of many traditional Pembrokeshire cottages with cement-washed roofs to be seen *en route*, bear right, signposted Abercastle, and follow the more important branch to the seaside hamlet. On the way, you will cross a crossroads and head past two minor T-junctions before descending into the steep-sided inlet of Abercastle.
2. The steep drop down into the attractive hamlet is matched by a stiff pull out again, as far as the trackway leading to Longhouse farm. A brief diversion (on foot, please, as this lane only has footpath, not bridleway, status) down the farm lane takes you to Carreg Sampson burial chamber.
3. Back on the road, continue south-westwards to Tre-fin. Head straight on at the T-junction on the outskirts of the village, following the signs to Llanrhian.
4. In the centre of the village, bear right at the central 'green' of bedrock, and follow the wide main street, signposted to Llanrhian and St Davids, past the inn and weaving centre. After a steepish drop and climb, past the site of Melin Tre-fin, follow the lane, ignoring two side turns, into Llanrhian. Llanrhian Church tower is 13th century, but the church itself was rebuilt and restored in the 19th century. At the crossroads, take the lane signposted to Whitesand.
5. Providing you do not yield to the temptations of Trevaccoon (Trefacwn) farm's cream teas, this road will take you on to another crossroads. Turn right, signposted to Abereiddi, and follow the lane to the beach, old quarries and ruined street. An ice cream van is often to be found here, in season.

6. After exploring Abereiddi, follow the lane for about 100 yards, to a T-junction. Turn right and climb ¾ mile past two farms to a second T-junction. Turn right again. Follow the lane past Berea chapel to a third T-junction. Turn left, signposted to Llandigige Fawr, and follow a narrow winding lane which heads across a stretch of rough moorland, with views over Carn Penbiri and Carn Llidi on your right. At the next T-junction, turn left to Carnhedryn, past a house that looks like a chapel, and a half-ruined farm. On reaching the main road, turn left and then right some 100 yards further on, opposite the old school. The narrow lane is signposted to Skyfog. Although the word is a particularly ugly Anglicisation of the Welsh name Ysgeifiog, it may well describe the weather hereabouts in winter! Follow the lane past the turn for Ysgeifiog, over a picturesque bridge across the River Solva (a mere brook) and up to the crossroads near Kingheriot Farm, an attractive and substantial farmhouse. The buildings seen on the horizon along this stretch are part of the military base at Brawdy. Turn left at the Kingheriot crossroads and follow the narrow, winding and occasionally grass-centred lane past Tremaenhir and its standing stones to another crossroads.

7. Turn left at the crossroads, signposted to Croesgoch, and follow the road to a T-junction some 400 yards further on. Bear right, signposted to Llandeloy, and, ignoring a junction on your right, follow the lane for some 600 yards to a T-junction, where you turn left, signposted to Croesgoch. Follow the lane for some 1,200 yards to a T-junction at a sharp bend in the road. Bear right, i.e. head straight on and follow the unsigned minor road to the hamlet of Treffynnon.

8. At the T-junction turn left. About 50 yards further on, turn right at another T-junction, taking the minor road signposted to Mathry. Follow the minor road all the way back to the start of the route, crossing the B4330 and the A487, as well as the infant Western Cleddau (Cleddau Wen) river on the way. The final one mile climb up to the church is, I warn you, quite tough on both legs and lungs!

A solitary fishing boat on the Western Cleddau (Ride 15).

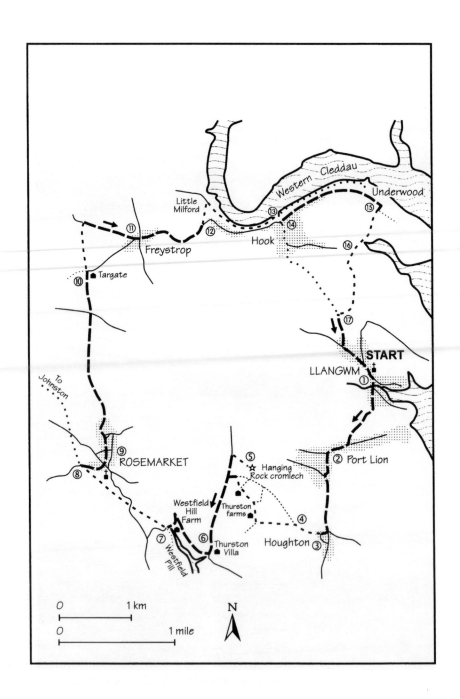

15 Rough Stuff Around Llangwm

Fact File

Distance:	11½ miles (18.5 km)
Time:	4-5 hours
Maps:	OS Landranger 158 Tenby & surrounding area or 157 St Davids and Haverfordwest; OS Pathfinder 1080 Narberth and 1104 Tenby and Saundersfoot; OS Outdoor Leisure 36 South Pembrokeshire
Start:	Llangwm church SM 990093
Terrain:	Quiet lanes, rough bridlepaths, green lanes and foreshore track. Very muddy in places.
Refreshments:	Llangwm: shops and Cottage Inn Rosemarket: Huntsman Inn Hook: New Anchor Inn
Parking:	See Start
Gates:	9
Suitable for:	Those looking for a rough, tough, muddy and enjoyable ride, taking in attractive and varied countryside.
Note:	Part of this ride can be affected by tidal flooding. Check your tide tables before setting out or, alternatively, use the rather less interesting diversion from Hook to Llangwm, which also cuts out most of the roughest riding.

Along the way

Although this ride will appeal to those who enjoy very rough off-road cycling, the less adventurous will also find much of interest and can avoid the roughest and, perhaps, most interesting, not to say fun section by taking the high-tide diversion, no matter what state the ride is in.

As much of the off-road riding on this route is through a Site of Special Scientific Interest, perhaps 'rough stuff', although describing the terrain well, is not an ideal title for this ride.

97

The site is a sensitive habitat and cyclists should respect the environment.

There are historic, prehistoric, as well as more modern sites of interest *en route*. Hanging Stone cromlech, for example, shows that this area has been inhabited since the Stone Age and, although overgrown and neglected, this burial chamber, part of which has been incorporated into a hedge, is very evocative.

For a description of Rosemarket, Houghton and Neyland and interesting sites in the vicinity of the three settlements, including Westfield Pill Nature Reserve, see Ride 4: Brunel Cycle Route, p. 19.

The National Trust land of Little Milford Wood, through which the route descends to the Western Cleddau estuary, was once an extensive area of coppiced oak woods. Coppicing on a commercial basis ceased in the 1920s and some sections were cleared and planted with conifers about 50 years ago. In 1975 the woods were left to the National Trust, who are thinning out the conifers to allow natural regeneration of the native hardwood species. The woods also contain evidence of medieval surface mining and were part of the large Freystrop Colliery which produced good quality anthracite for export around the world. Production was at its peak in 1934 when 42,000 tons of coal were raised. The mine closed in 1948 and by today little remains to be seen. Also within this delightful woodland are the three springs that used to be the village water supply. The woods now have numerous walks and bridlepaths for quiet enjoyment.

Hook is now quiet and peaceful, belying its industrial past. The New Anchor Inn, converted to a pub in the 1960s, replaced the Anchor Inn, one of the buildings near the shores of the estuary. Despite its short history, it's claimed that the new inn has a resident poltergeist!

The section of the Western Cleddau visited on this ride, was once a busy commercial artery: boats full of coal from local mines and limestone from neighbouring quarries were transported via the waterway, which in later years was also a base for RAF flying boats. Today, however, it is mainly used for recreation, and is part of an important wildfowl sanctuary where you can see redshank, dunlin, shelduck and teal, among other species. It is a naturalist's paradise. The traditional method of compass fishing, which involves attaching a net between two long poles, is still used to catch salmon on the river and both boats and nets are often seen moored by the side of the shore.

Llangwm, once isolated on its landward side by poor roads, was not always the quiet village of today. Coal was formerly exported from Sprinkle Pill and Llangwm Pill and the village's isolation, combined with the hard life of the residents, gave Llangwm a reputation for having aggressive inhabitants, the women being worse than the men. In the 19th century a haymaker was stabbed during an after-work drinking session and this gave the landowner—a total abstainer—the excuse he needed to close the village pub. The village remained dry until 1953 when a bakehouse was converted into the Cottage Club, where locals could once again buy intoxicating drinks. It is now a fully operational pub.

Route

1. From the car park near the church, turn right, head down the hill and across the bridge over Llangwm Pill, and climb out of the village up Butter Hill.
2. At the second T-junction, situated at the top of the hill—beyond Foxhill and about ¾ mile from the start—turn left to join New Wells Road, signposted to Burton. After some 300 yards, turn left again and follow the lane for approximately 800 yards to a staggered crossroads by the school in Houghton.
3. Turn right, and head between Jubilee Play Park and the school. As the lane swings left, turn right again and follow a broad, rough track, boasting footpath, bridleway and cycle route signs. This is part of the Brunel Cycle Route. Follow this for about 450 yards to where a large bridle-way sign points the way off the track and over a wooden bridge into the trees beyond.

4. Here you start a section of rough cycling, often wet and muddy, made rough by horses, a bit overgrown and great fun. This winds westwards and all too soon becomes a good track, heading past the front of some cottages and Upper and Lower Thurston farms, beyond which is a T-junction with a lane. Go right and continue uphill for 200 yards to where a partially concreted track comes in from the right, signposted to Hanging Rock Cromlech.
5. Walk down the track (footpath only) to the cromlech, which is visible against the left-hand hedge of the field ahead, just beyond the point where the track swings right.
6. After viewing the cromlech, retrace your steps to the lane and turn left, enjoying the downhill ride, past the turn to the Thurston farms and on to a T-junction near Thurston Villa. Turn right at the T-junction, climb up a short but very steep rise and on towards a T-junction about half a mile further on, just past Westfield Hill farm. Turn left and continue down a rough, concrete-surfaced lane. Cross Westfield Pill and climb a few yards to the old Great Western Railway line. Westfield Pill Nature Reserve is on your left and part of the Brunel Cycle Route on your right.
7. Turn right through the first of many ingenious bike stiles, called more properly a Pembrokeshire Bicycle Gate, designed to allow cycle access but to exclude motorbikes and horses. Follow the old railway line through a delightful little wooded valley, which, in season, is ablaze with flowers. At one point the route, which is for the most part good, takes you across a bridge over a road and, further on, passes under the remains of a hill-top fort, but both are hard to see through the trees.
8. After about a mile you come to a road where you have the choice of: *either* crossing over and continuing along the railway to Johnston and back again (adding 3½ miles to you day), *or* turning right in order to follow the lane which climbs to Rosemarket. Johnston was once a poor hamlet but, having grown following the arrival of the railway, is now a thriving village with its own station.

On reaching Rosemarket, turn right at the T-junction,

then immediately left, up Middle Street, signposted to Haverfordwest and Johnston. Ignore the cycle route signs.

9. Follow Middle Street for approximately 400 yards, to a T-junction near a chapel. Turn left, and head along the lane, signposted to Johnston, for a little over a mile to a crossroads. Go straight over the crossroads and down a lane, signposted to Freystrop and as being Unsuitable for Long Vehicles.

10. After about 600 yards, by the buildings at Targate, the lane takes a 90° turn to the right and a farm drive joins from the left. The route goes straight on, along a rough, muddy bridle path for 400 yards, then crosses a ford before heading up to a house called Fiddlers Green, where the track improves again and leads to a T-junction. Turn right and follow the minor road to Freystrop.

11. Turn left at the T-junction by the telephone box, cross the main road and head along New Road, signposted to Hook. Follow this winding lane to the National Trust car park, just beyond the Hook village sign.

12. Here you have a choice: *either* continue along the lane past the pub, as far as the T-junction by a chapel in Hook, *or* take the track by the National Trust information board and follow it down through the woods to enjoy a fun ride along the muddy shoreline track. The shoreline RUPP (Road used as Public Path) may soon be reclassified as a bridleway but this should not affect cyclists' rights to ride this track.

The off-road option takes you down a steep, rough and often very muddy track between coppiced oak and conifer woods to a T-junction near some buildings. Turn right and follow the track which runs behind a house and onto the foreshore beyond two buildings, one of which was once a pub. Check your tidetables before riding this section, which rewards you with superb views of the estuary. Often flooded and in places unridable, even at low tide, this track is followed for about half a mile to a point where it climbs into the trees to join another rough track. (Technically it is possible to follow the foreshore track all the way to Underwood but perhaps enough is enough . . .)

13. Turn right and follow the zigzag track up to the lane at Greenway Close, in Hook. Turn left and follow the lane to a T-junction by a chapel.
14. At the T-junction by the chapel in Hook you again have a choice. If you wish to avoid some of the roughest and muddiest cycling, or if the tide is in, turn right and follow the lane, signposted to Llangwm, all the way back to the start of the ride. Alternatively, and providing you have checked the tide tables, gird your loins and take the dead-end road, signposted Lower Quay Road, to your left. Follow the dead-end road to its end, just over a mile further on, passing the track up from Underwood where those who may have followed the full extent of the foreshore will drip their muddy way up to join the route.
15. At the end of the road near some ruined buildings, a farm drive heads left but our route goes straight on through the gate and along a green lane signposted as a bridleway. As it approaches the shoreline again, this muddy trackway becomes a fully-fledged stream! On reaching the shore, turn right and cross a deep tidal ford—impassable at high tide, muddy at low tide and *very* slippery—to gain a track which heads into a lane.
16. Turn left and, where the lane comes to an end, take the muddy bridlepath to the left of the house. This path leads you down to a ford and pony gate, and into a field up which you climb to the top left-hand corner and another pony gate.

    Go through the gate and follow the left-hand hedge to another pony gate which heads into a green lane. Follow the lane for about a quarter of a mile to a T-junction of green lanes. Turn right in order to join the minor road by Llangwm cemetery.

    It sounds fairly straightforward but, in all but the driest weather, it is tough cycling. Furthermore, in summer it may be rather overgrown. However, this challenging section of the route is worth trying for its scenic rewards.
17. On reaching the minor road, turn left and follow it to the start of the ride in Llangwm.

Llangwm Church (Ride 15).

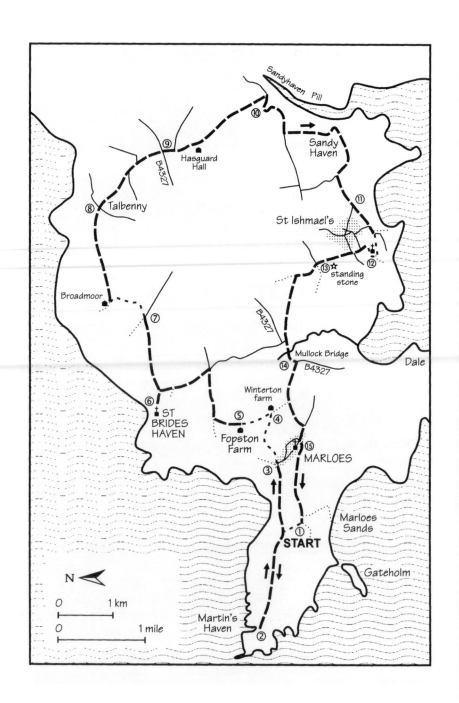

16 Marloes and St Brides

Fact File

Distance:	19 miles (30.5 km)
Time:	5-6 hours
Maps:	OS Landranger 158 St Davids & Haverfordwest; OS Outdoor Leisure 36 South Pembrokeshire
Start:	Marloes Sands car park SM 780082
Nearest Towns:	Haverfordwest and Milford Haven
Terrain:	Mainly quiet lanes and good tracks. Some off-road sections can be muddy and some roads can be busy at the height of the tourist season.
Refreshments:	Marloes: Post Office shop, Lobster Pot Inn and Foxes Inn St Ishmaels: Brook Inn Martin's Haven: ice cream van (seasonal)
Parking:	See Start
Gates:	5, and one stile
Suitable for:	All the family, though care must be taken on some road sections.
Cycle Hire:	Broad Haven and Dale

Along the way

A quick look at the map will indicate that this area, the site of two disused airfields, is one of the flatter parts of Pembrokeshire. Despite this, the Marloes and St Brides peninsula is not only full of interest, but also offers a couple of climbs and free-wheeling descents.

An important area for early man, the region has a generous scattering of Mesolithic, Bronze and Iron Age sites, as well as places associated with the lives of Celtic saints. At The Nab Head, on the coast west of St Brides, there is the site of a Mesolithic chipping floor where, approximately 10,000 years ago, flint tools were fashioned and, occasionally, worked fragments of this glass-sharp rock are still to be found. A fine Bronze Age standing stone near Mabesgate, about 10ft high, 7ft wide, but less than 12 inches thick, is one of the tallest in south-west Wales. A 'knife blade' type stone of laminated sandstone, it is a spectacular example of a triangular standing stone.

The headland west of Martin's Haven, known as the Deer Park, was fortified in the Iron Age, though the planned Deer Park, part of the Kensington estate, never saw any deer.

Martin's Haven is the embarkation point for boat trips to Skomer National Nature Reserve, which is especially rich in sea birds and Iron Age remains, while the sea area around Skomer and the Deer Park has been designated a Marine Nature Reserve, the first of its kind in Britain. Martin's Haven is often busy with divers and visitors to the islands preparing to set off for their respective wet and dry nature studies! Sheltered from south-westerly storms, Martin's Haven has long been an important site, and when the public toilets were being built in the 1980s, a 7th- to 9th-century stone with a carved ring cross was unearthed. Now set into the wall, this stone may have been a pilgrim's prayer stone marker, or an indicator of a Celtic burial site. As well as the aforementioned toilets, you will find in Martin's Haven a display providing information on the nature reserves, which is well worth studying.

Other interesting sites nearby include Gateholm Island, with its remains of an early medieval settlement of over 100 huts. Amongst the finds were Roman coins, a bronze pin of 6th to 9th-century style and French ceramic ware. St Brides was possibly the site of an early Christian settlement. St Bride was a contemporary of St David who, according to one tradition, set sail with some 'devout women' and founded a nunnery in Ireland. Others would claim that she never left her native Ireland. Her reputation, however, spread far and wide and in addition to the 16 churches dedicated to her memory in Wales, others are found in Cornwall, Brittany and Italy. There used to be an earlier, small chapel at the head of the sheltered haven but when it fell out of use, it was put into service as a salt house for the herring trade. This blasphemous use caused dire retribution: the herrings deserted the coastal waters and the chapel fell into the sea—'When St Brides chapel a salt house was made, St Brides lost the herring trade.'

The erosion that destroyed the chapel has also, on occasions, exposed small stone 6th- to 10th-century coffins some 10-20 yards north of the limekiln. St Bride seems to have taken her revenge in good measure!

Other than the Celtic-style church dedicated to St Bridget, belying the site's early importance, there are few buildings in and around St Brides Haven. Overlooking the inlet, however, is the imposing cliff-top mansion once owned by John de St Bride, a supporter of Henry III, and the one-time family seat of the Barony of Kensington. Once a hospital, this grand pile is now divided into holiday flats.

Marloes has an interesting history. Despite its distance from the sea, it was, in the past, predominantly a fishing village. The sea-going tradition persists but it is now mainly connected with lobster fishing and taking visitors out to the islands. In the past the villagers were fishermen and smallholders grazing their cattle on the wide moorland held in common. However, Lord Kensington enclosed the common in 1847, depriving the fishermen/smallholders of half their living. Despite the fact that most of the enclosed land reverted to moorland, the community never really recovered from this blow, although the farms today are large and prosperous and are renowned for their early potatoes. Lord Kensington could not have been a popular sort, as in the 19th century he closed all the village pubs and Marloes was dry until 1963, when the Lobster Pot Inn (twinned with the Lobster Pot Inn in Carne, Ireland) was opened.

Nearby Marloes Sands, a good sandy beach backed by cliffs, noted for their near vertical layers of rock, is well worth a visit for a swim after a day's cycling.

St Ishmael's boasts an old motte to the north of the village, but of more interest is the fascinating church tucked away in a valley whose sides are partially clothed with wind-sculpted trees. The churchyard is in two parts, being linked by a bridge across the stream that flows down to Monk Haven. Set in a beautiful spot, the church repays a visit and holds some interesting icons and a model of the church, made of matches. To avoid the dangerous passage around the Pembrokeshire coast, a road, perhaps even used from Stone Age times but more probably by Christians and medieval pilgrims, links Monk Haven with St Davids. Traces of old religious buildings are still to be found but the wall across the shore is 18th century and the tower merely a folly. To the north-east and to the west of the quiet village, standing stones testify to man's early presence in the area. West of St Ishmael's is the now disused Dale airfield.

The route from near Dale to Mullock Bridge follows the line Henry Tudor must have taken when he landed on the Dale peninsula, on his way from Brittany to defeat Richard III at Bosworth Field in 1485.

The islands and cliffed coastline, in particular, are of international importance. The whole area is renowned for its flora and fauna, and the sections near the cliffs for their breeding colonies of sea birds. Marloes Mere, near the car park at the start of the ride, is important both for its visiting birds and varied aquatic animal and plants. St Brides Haven and Martin's Haven are the places to watch for seals and dolphins, while the route will reward you with superb views of the coast and inland scenery. The hedgerows are full of flowers in season, so look out for gorse, violets, red campion, bluebells and primroses, among others.

This cycle route follows some of the 'on-road' sections of the Pembrokeshire Coast Path, the long-distance trail from St Dogmaels to Amroth, and along these stretches of road rucksack-laden walkers are as much a hazard to cyclists as cars!

Route

1. From the car park head north-west on a rough track for some 300 yards to join the minor road linking Marloes with Martin's Haven.
2. Turn left to visit Martin's Haven, a mile down the lane, then retrace your route and head for Marloes.
3. On entering the village you will see a small triangular green with flower beds and a bench on the left-hand side of the road, with the old village pump just beyond. Turn

left and follow the track, signposted as a bridleway, north of the green, bearing right in front of a cottage and heading roughly north-east. The track zigzags past the old school, now a private house, and becomes a green lane as it approaches Winterton.

4. On reaching the farm, do not go through the main farmyard but turn hard left through a gate and follow a faint track diagonally across the field, in a north-westerly direction, to a gate near some low buildings. Continue down the next field, again diagonally, to Fopston Farm.

5. From the farm, follow the surfaced access drive to the crossroads near the grandly-named Kensington Place. Turn left and head along the quiet lane to the T-junction, strangely called St Brides Cross. Turn left at the telephone box and follow the lane signposted as a dead end and as Unsuitable for Coaches, to visit St Brides Haven.

6. From St Brides Haven, return to St Brides Cross and head straight on, following the lane signposted to Haverfordwest as far as the point where it turns sharp right at Upper Ripperston Farm.

7. Head along the track straight ahead of you, signposted to Mill Haven and as Unsuitable for Motors. In the field on the left are the almost invisible remains of an ancient enclosure. The track soon becomes a green lane which leads to Lower Broadmoor farm. At the farm, turn right and follow the well-surfaced access lane which leads past Middle and Upper Broadmoor to a crossroads at Cross Farm, Talbenny. To your right are the remains of an airfield and over the next few miles, you pass many old wartime buildings once associated with the airfield, but now used for more peaceful purposes.

8. At the crossroads go straight on along the lane signposted to Hasguard Cross. In places, the road still retains its wartime concrete surface, when it was used as a taxiway by the planes. Ignore all side turns until you reach Hasguard Cross crossroads.

9. Go straight over the crossroads and down the lane, signposted to Milford Haven and Sandy Hill chapel. Follow the lane south-eastwards for about 1½ miles,

passing Hasguard Hall and Upper and Lower Hasguard, to a major T-junction above Sandyhaven Pill.

10. At the T-junction, turn right, and head downhill past the chapel and up a steep hill to another T-junction, where you turn left along a lane signposted to Sandy Haven. The lane, which is a bit of a switchback ride, heads past several farms and, ignoring the dead-end turn by the limekiln at Sandy Farm, brings you up to a T-junction some 1¼ miles further on. At the junction, turn left, signposted to St Ishmael's.

11. About half a mile down this lane, a little way beyond some playing fields, turn left and head along dead-end Lindsway Road. Follow the road past some houses and a turn to Monkhill Farm, to where the surfaced lane swings left through a gate, signposted Private Road. At this point, go straight on through the gate and into a field. Although this faint track is waymarked as a footpath, at present, it is a RUPP (Road used as Public Path) and you have every right to cycle along it. The track follows the hedge on your left-hand side to the corner of the field, then drops down over a stile which is rather awkward, before continuing alongside the church-yard wall to meet a lane by the charming and ancient church.

12. Follow the lane around the church and up out of the valley. Head straight on at the first T-junction, right at the second and left at the third, signposted to Dale and Haverfordwest. A little beyond a nursery, the Mabesgate standing stone is hidden behind a large shed in a field to your left.

13. Ignoring the first T-junction beyond the standing stone, continue along the lane to a T-junction at Mabesgate. At the houses, turn left and enjoy a downhill run for approximately 1½ miles to a T-junction on the far side of Mullock Bridge. At Mullock Bridge, the old and new bridge stand alongside one another: the new bridge cuts out an interesting wiggle in the road.

14. At the T-junction turn right, signposted to Marloes and Martin's Haven, and climb up a pleasant valley, ignoring side turns, until you reach Marloes church.

15. Turn left at the church, signposted to Marloes Sands and the Youth Hostel, and follow the lane back to the car park at the start of the ride.

Monk Haven Church (Ride 16).

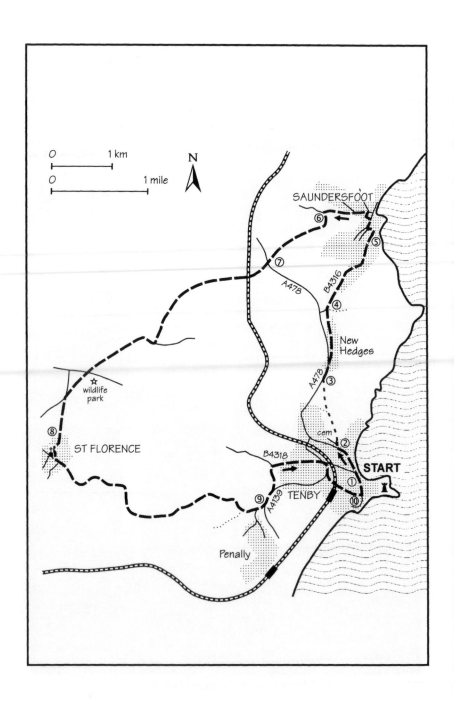

17 Tenby, Saundersfoot and St Florence

Fact File

Distance:	13 miles (20.9 km)
Time:	3-4 hours
Maps:	OS Pathfinder 1125 Manorbier and Tenby; OS Landranger 158 Tenby & surrounding area; OS Outdoor Leisure 36 South Pembrokeshire
Start:	Tenby Tourist Information Centre, The Croft SN 132007
Nearest Town:	Tenby
Terrain:	Mainly quiet lanes. One section of off-road riding is slippery when wet, but not too rough. Some short stretches on main roads are busy in the holiday season.
Refreshments:	Tenby and Saundersfoot: everything you need St Florence: several pubs and a shop
Parking:	Good parking facilities in Tenby, though these may fill up at the height of the tourist season.
Suitable for:	Family cycling, if care is taken and close supervision given to younger cyclists on busy road sections.
Cycle Hire:	Bro Bikes, Upper Frog Street, Tenby, Tel: 01834 844766

Along the way

All three centres visited on this route, Tenby, Saundersfoot and St Florence, have long and fascinating histories and good books and leaflets, recalling their past and particular points of interest, are available at Tenby Tourist Information Centre.

Tenby, a major tourist centre which attracts crowds of visitors every summer, is justly famous for its beaches as well as the attractions of the walled town itself. Castle Hill was more than likely the site of a Bronze Age fort, although later defences have obliterated any traces of an earlier structure. In the 9th century, an anonymous Welsh poet described the fort at Dinbych

113

Saundersfoot harbour (Ride 17).

Flemish chimney, St Florence (Ride 17).

(Little Fort) as a fine fortress, overlooking a sheltered and well protected harbour. During the 9th and 10th centuries Vikings raided the Pembrokeshire shore and some will tell you that Tenby (an Anglicised version of the Welsh name Dinbych), was their raiding base.

In the 11th century the Normans took control of the area, dispossessing the Welsh and establishing a powerful defensive position held by the earls of Pembroke. With Tenby defending their eastern flank, the Normans could bring in large numbers of Norman, English, French and Flemish settlers to Pembrokeshire, thereby laying the foundations of 'little England beyond Wales'. This is not to say they had it all their own way, with Welsh warriors battering and even seizing town and castle in 1153, 1187 and in 1260 when Llywelyn ap Gruffydd 'put the town to the sword' as a protest against the Norman occupation of Wales. To avoid any repetition of such mayhem, Tenby had new walls, towers and gates built to enclose the town with impregnable defences, backed by the cliff-top fort. It is these defences, still remarkably complete, that gird the centre of the town. However, the North Gate was demolished in the 1700s to improve traffic flow, and later the West Gate had additional access arches constructed to create the present five arches.

During the 15th century extra defences were built on the seaward side of the town, but these were on a smaller scale than the massive landward defences. The medieval defences were never put to the test—despite some close calls—while the castle itself fell into disrepair from as early as 1377.

During the Civil War, Tenby stood for Parliament and was taken by Royalist forces in 1643, but fell to Parliamentarians in 1644, after a heavy bombardment by artillery—a weapon the defences were never designed to withstand. In 1648 Royalists again held Tenby, but only for a short while before surrendering.

During the 13th century Tenby was not only a fishing port but also traded with Brittany, Spain, Ireland and Devon. However, by the 16th century it was trading mainly with Bristol. Despite being a rich town in Tudor times, by the 17th century the settlement fell into decline and poverty, as a consequence of war, plague and competition for fish markets with Brixham and Dartmouth. In 1788 Tenby was described as 'the most complete

116

ruins of an old town': two-thirds was either in ruins or had vanished completely. By the end of the 18th century, however, sea bathing had become a popular pastime amongst aristocratic patrons who had 'discovered' Tenby and its beaches. By 1800, poverty was almost a thing of the past and Tenby the holiday resort was born. The town developed throughout the Victorian era, joining the railway network in 1866 and gaining a pier in 1897.

The industrial communities of South Wales, exploiting the rail links established in the 1860s, found Tenby to their taste and allowed the town the opportunity to cater for their needs, grow rich and more popular than ever. Today, Tenby is a very popular holiday resort catering for all tastes, its economy dependent upon the maintenance of visitor numbers.

Much of the town's history is reflected in its architecture for within its bounds are medieval walls, a Tudor Merchant's House, Georgian facades and Victorian hotels, and modern tourist and leisure facilities, all of which are worthy of attention during a prolonged visit. The Church of St Marys in the centre of the town is a lovely building, light and airy with a superb ceiling, fine stained glass and intriguing memorials.

Saundersfoot, on the coast north of Tenby, has an entirely different history. What is now a pleasant tourist resort developed as a centre of the coal industry. Although the area was thinly populated from the Stone Age onward, and despite the presence of a Norman church and a nearby medieval castle/fortified manor, Saundersfoot originally referred to a property not a village: Saundersfoot Farm was a holding incorporating a few coal-pits. Coal mining is recorded as far back as 1324, but the industry developed during the 18th century and by 1801 St Issells was one of the most densely populated parishes in rural Pembrokeshire.

In 1829 the establishment of the Saundersfoot Railway and Harbour Company was authorised by Parliament in order to promote the export of coal by sea. In 1837 five jetties were in full use exporting coal to southern and eastern England (coal for breweries), Cornwall, France, Germany and even Scandinavia. Iron from the nearby Stepaside Ironworks and bricks from Wiseman's Bridge also passed through the port and expanding village of Saundersfoot.

Water pumps, Tavernspite (Ride 18).

Boat and ship, St Bride's Bay (Ride 16).

In addition to the industrial activity, from the 1850s onward Saundersfoot received a growing number of summer visitors, thanks to the increasing popularity of seaside holidays and the arrival of the Great Western Railway in 1866. With the decline of the coal industry in the 20th century due to geological difficulties, and the closure of the last working mine in 1939 (a small private mine was periodically worked up to the 1950s), Saundersfoot with its fine beach and good harbour has become a residential village and holiday resort, its picturesque setting belying its industrial past.

St Florence, an attractive and seductive village, has an interesting history dating back to the Bronze and Iron Age. The Normans settled here around AD 1100 and were responsible for Anglicising the population.

Farming has long been the main employment of St Florence, though until an embankment was flung across the mouth of the tidal Ritec or Rhyd-deg (Fair Ford) stream to reclaim the land for agriculture, the estuary was wide enough for ships to sail up as far as the old corn mill, now a ruin and picnic site. A large stone set in the earth by the 'Ark', opposite the shop, is said to have been used for tying up ships, though this is unlikely to have been its original position.

St Florence has six listed buildings, some with Flemish chimneys although they are not, in fact, of Flemish origin. The chimneys are very much a local architectural feature and often a late addition to larger houses. The fascinating church was established in the 12th century, enlarged in the 13th century, and the tower was added in the 16th century. Refurbished in 1997, the church has a very different appearance and a calm atmosphere. An ancient preaching cross also stands in the churchyard.

The roads and lanes linking Tenby, Saundersfoot and St Florence—three very different communities—offer good views over the rolling south Pembrokeshire countryside, except where high hedges full of wild flowers intrude. The area is noted for the Tenby Daffodil (*Narcissus pseudonarcissus* subsp *obvallaris*), a small, strongly-coloured native species. Between 1883 and 1885 about half a million bulbs of this flower were dug up and exported to London, an act which almost led to the extinction of the distinctive local flower. Fortunately, the Tenby Daffodil is re-establishing itself, although it is not too common even around its old home town.

To do justice to this attractive part of Pembrokeshire would take several books on history, architecture, flora and fauna and I heartily recommend you buy some of the selection available locally.

Route

1. From Tenby Tourist Information Centre, head back up The Croft and at the T-junction, turn right and follow The Norton (A478) for about 450 yards to a small T-junction where a minor road, Mayfield Drive, joins The Norton.
2. Turn up Mayfield Drive, signposted to the Aquarium, and at the fork almost immediately ahead, bear right and follow this quiet lane past the cemetery. Beyond the cemetery gates, follow the rough track surfaced with well-polished hard-core that is lumpy when dry and slippery as ice when wet. As the track is lined with nettles, care is needed to avoid unpleasant spills. At a fork in this bridle-way, ½ mile beyond the aquarium turn, bear right. Ahead, the track improves and becomes a well-surfaced lane leading down to the busy A478.
3. Taking great care, turn right at the main road, then right again, about 250 yards ahead, just beyond the little corrugated iron St Annes Church, and follow the road signposted to New Hedges and Rowston Park camp site. Since the A478 is very busy in the tourist season, you are advised not to cross and re-cross the road, but rather to push your bike along the verge from the lane to the turn to New Hedges. This is an especially good idea if you are accompanied by young children.
4. Climb through New Hedges, past shops and a pub, to a T-junction. Turn right and head along the B4316 and enjoy a marvellous one mile free-wheeling run to the entrance of Saundersfoot Harbour car park.

Lime kilns at Solva harbour (Ride 24).

Sea front at Amroth (Ride 18).

5. At Saundersfoot Harbour car park, the route goes left along the one-way system (or you can dismount and explore the village and harbour first) before swinging right, uphill to a crossroads where you turn left into The Ridgeway. Follow The Ridgeway for some 100 yards to a junction (just short of a Wesleyan chapel) where you turn left down Westfield Road.
6. Follow Westfield Road for approximately half a mile to a T-junction opposite The Incline Cottage. At the cottage, turn sharp left and begin a longish but not too steep a climb of about one mile up to a crossroads with the A478. Remember the descent you enjoyed down to the harbour? Now it is payback time!
7. With care, cross the A478 and head into Devonshire Drive, a superb 2½ mile ride along a quiet lane which, ignoring all side turns, takes you down to a crossroads by Manor House Wildlife Park. Go straight over the crossroads and follow a small lane, signposted to St Florence. At the next junction, turn left, signposted to Manorbier, Lamphey and St Florence, and continue into St Florence.
8. The road leads you down a one-way system around the church, to a T-junction with Cross Street. Turn left, signposted to Penally, and follow the zigzagging lane for about 3¾ miles, past a charming old mill and picnic site, over the Ritec stream, across farmland and back down to the Ritec, near a fishery and wetland site.
9. At a T-junction beyond the entrance to a golf course, turn left and at the T-junction with the A4139, turn left again. About 400 yards further on, turn left at a T-junction near the Welcome to Tenby sign. Follow the minor road for about 500 yards to a T-junction. Turn right at the junction and follow Heywood Lane (B4318), signposted to Tenby, Cardigan, Carmarthen and Saundersfoot, for about one-third of a mile—ignoring side turns and following Town Centre signs—down to a T-junction with the main road. Turn right and at the roundabouts follow the Town Centre signs uphill under the railway viaduct. Continue straight on at all junctions and follow South Parade and St Florence

Parade along the outer side of the old town walls, past the Five Arches, in the direction of the esplanade.

10. Just before the one-way system swings right along the esplanade, turn left, head through the old town wall, by the Imperial Hotel, then left and on to a crossroads. Turn right and go along St Georges Street, past the churchyard, and up Church Street to Tudor Square. Turn left and head up The Norton, following signs for the Information Centre, for a quick return to the start of the ride. Alternatively, you may wish to turn right and visit the harbour and Castle Hill before returning up Bridge Street as far as Quay Hill. Turn up Quay Hill to visit the Tudor Merchant's House before continuing your journey along Crackwell Street, above North Beach, and The Norton back to the start of the ride at the Tourist Information Centre on The Croft.

I recommend you get off your bike and walk through the town streets. This allows access to one-way streets and ease of passage through the summer crowds. But a full exploration of the town, and its maze of intriguing streets, lanes and passages is best done once you have put your bike away for the day.

Cycling to Pentre Ifan (Ride 21).

Wolfscastle Bridge (Ride 25).

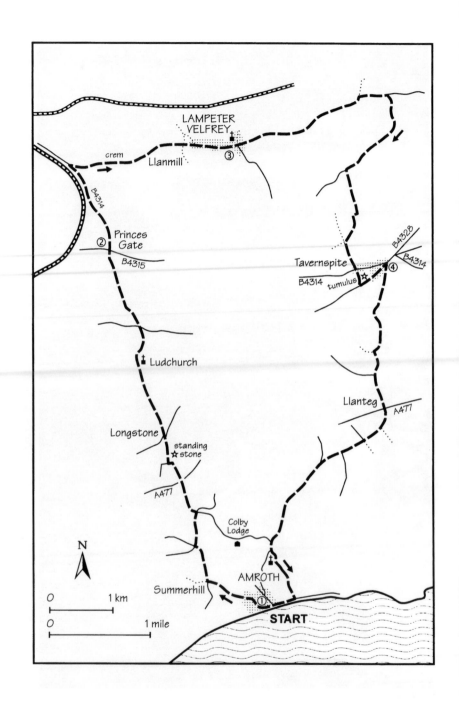

LAMPETER
VELFREY

crem
Llanmill
③

B4314

Princes
Gate
②
B4315

Tavernspite
B4328

B4314

B4314 tumulus ☆ ④

Ludchurch

Llanteg
A477

Longstone
☆ standing
stone

A477

Colby
Lodge

N

Summerhill
AMROTH
①

START

O   1 km

O   1 mile

18 Amroth and Lampeter Velfry

Fact File

Distance:	16 miles (25.7 km)
Time:	4-5 hours
Maps:	OS Landranger 158 Tenby & surrounding area; OS Outdoor Leisure 36 South Pembrokeshire
Start:	Amroth car park SN 163070
Nearest Towns:	Tenby and Narberth
Terrain:	Mainly quiet lanes and minor roads; some sections on B roads. A roller-coaster ride through undulating countryside. Very little flat riding.
Refreshments:	Amroth: Amroth Arms, Temple Bar Inn and various shops Summerhill: shop Tavernspite: Alpha Inn Llanteglos: The Hunting Lodge
Parking:	See Start
Suitable for:	The fitter cyclist who can cope with many hills. During the high season many of the normally quiet roads may become busy. Take care crossing the A477.

Along the way

Amroth, a small village, popular with holiday-makers, is perhaps best known for being the southern terminus of the Pembrokeshire Coast Path, the Knights Way and Landsker Trail than for any major feature. However, Amroth too has its attractions for the discerning, and a long history: it boasts two castles and several nearby prehistoric sites. The original castle—a motte near the church—lies a short distance outside the village, whilst the 'modern' castle is an 18th-century building on the site of a 14th-century fortress of which only a much-restored gateway remains.

Nearby Colby Lodge, now owned by the National Trust, was designed by the architect John Nash and built in the 1700s. It is situated in a delightful wooded valley and its gardens, noted for their rhododendrons and hydrangeas, are open to the public. For those with an interest in far more ancient sites and sights, the Coal Measure mudstones exposed in the cliffs between Amroth and Wiseman's Bridge contain fossilized plants, while traces of a submerged forest are sometimes to be seen on the beach. Please do not remove fragments of the 6,000 year old submerged forest—leave it as it is for all to enjoy.

At Longstone, between Amroth and Ludchurch, you pass the Longstone standing stone, whilst near Tavernspite is Crug-y-swllt round barrow.

Lampeter Velfrey is an ancient site and has its share of earthworks. Near Pen Lan Farm, south-west at the village are the possible remains of three Stone Age chambered tombs.

Ludchurch was once a centre of limestone quarrying and lime burning, and although remains of the industry can still be seen, rural tranquility is the order of the present day.

There is a wonderful diversity of flora and fauna in the area covered by this ride, so nature lovers, as well as historians and those who enjoy good views and quiet roads, should all go home content after their day's cycling.

Route

1. From the free car park in Amroth, follow the sea-front road before turning right at the bottom of the long steep climb up to Summerhill. At the T-junction by the house with glorious stained-glass windows (a former chapel?) turn right, signposted to Tenby, Pembroke Dock and St Clears, and right again at the next crossroads, signposted to Ludchurch and St Clears. Some half a mile further on is another crossroads where you turn left, signposted to Ludchurch and Narberth, to cross the A477 via a bridge over a deep cutting. Continue along this quiet road, ignoring side turns,

through Longstone and Ludchurch: the solitary Longstone stands in an open field south of the hamlet, whilst the church at Ludchurch stands high on top of a crag overlooking a flooded limestone quarry, now a fishery.

2. About 1½ miles beyond the church is Princes Gate crossroads. Go straight over the B4315 and follow the B4314, signposted to the crematorium. About 1 mile north of Princes Gate, turn right off the B4314 and follow a minor road signposted to the crematorium and Lampeter Velfrey. Beyond the crematorium, the road narrows and is flanked by high hedge-banks as it dips and climbs by way of Llanmill to Lampeter Velfrey.

3. Opposite the church—a medieval building on a much more ancient site—are interpretation boards giving historical information about the area. Head straight on at the T-junction beyond the church and ignore all side turns until, after some half a mile, you turn right at a T-junction signposted to Tavernspite and coarse fishing. Follow this lane, past the fishery, for about 1¼ miles as far as a chapel at a T-junction. Turn left and climb to Tavernspite. This fairly strenuous climb brings you to a crossroads on the western outskirts of the village. Go straight over the B4314, past Crug-y-swllt tumulus (now a barely visible low mound) and at the T-junction, turn left.

Follow the road towards the centre of Tavernspite but turn right at the T-junction signposted to Llanteg. (This T-junction is just short of a more major junction with the B4314). The near corner of the junction is decorated with two 'village pumps'.

4. Ignoring side turns, follow this quiet, high-hedged lane to Llanteg. The roller-coaster ride comes to an abrupt halt at the crossroads where you encounter the fast and busy A477. Taking great care, head over the crossroads and follow the quiet road—ignoring all side turns—down to the coast, passing Amroth church on your right. At the T-junction on the sea-front, turn right and follow the coast road back to the start of the ride.

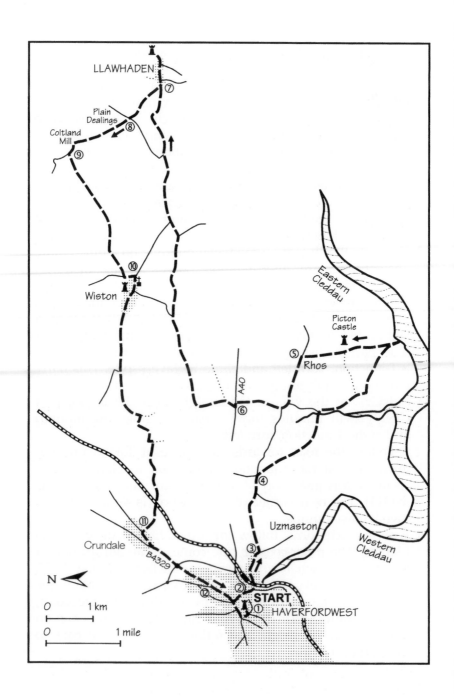

LLAWHADEN

Plain
Dealings

Coltland
Mill

⑦

⑧

⑨

Eastern
Cleddau

⑩

Wiston

Picton
Castle

⑤

Rhos

A40

⑥

④

Uzmaston

Western
Cleddau

⑪

Crundale

B4329

N

⑫

②

START

⑩

①

HAVERFORDWEST

O   1 km

O   1 mile

132

19 Haverfordwest and Llawhaden

Fact File

Distance:	23 miles (37 km)
Time:	5-6 hours (or all day if you visit all the sites *en route*)
Maps:	OS Landranger 158 Tenby & surrounding area; OS Outdoor Leisure 36 South Pembrokeshire
Start:	Haverfordwest castle SM 953157
Nearest Town:	Haverfordwest
Terrain:	Mainly quiet minor roads and lanes, though sections involving the crossing of the A40 and the B4329 can be busy. Haverfordwest is best traversed on foot or with great care, as the traffic can be heavy as you exit the town. Hills not too exhausting, but there are some short, sharp sections and long, easy gradients.
Refreshments:	Haverfordwest: everything available Picton Castle: restaurant and shop Crundale: General Picton pub
Parking:	Ample car parks dotted around Haverfordwest
Suitable for:	Those willing to brave busy sections of road to gain quiet countryside.
Note:	With the exception of Picton Castle, all the attractions mentioned are open Tuesday-Sunday inclusive, from April to October, 10.30 am to 5 pm or dusk, if earlier. Picton Castle is open on Thursdays and Sunday afternoons between July and September, as well as on Easter and Bank Holiday Sundays and Mondays. Admission charge, except to shop and restaurant.

Along the way

Haverfordwest (Hwlffordd), the county town of Pembrokeshire and the 'capital' of 'little England beyond Wales', is a truly fascinating town and is well worth taking the time to explore thoroughly. Although it may be on the site of an earlier settlement, nothing is known of Haverfordwest before the Normans came and built a castle early in the 12th century. The castle ruins, which dominate the skyline are pretty fragmentary when you get close to them: only the outer walls stand proud. Perhaps this is not too surprising, considering that Llywelyn Fawr (Llywelyn the Great) had a go at destroying it in 1220 when he put the town to the torch; it was ravaged by the supporters of Owain Glyndŵr in 1405, and Cromwell ordered it to be totally demolished in 1648.

None of these heroes succeeded in destroying the castle completely and, in its time, the site has served as a prison and police headquarters. More recently the former prison and Pembrokeshire Constabulary headquarters were converted to house the County Record Office and museum. The museum, now established in a house within the castle walls, is well worth a visit, and there are wonderful views of the countryside north of the town from the castle grounds.

The position of the town on the banks of the Western Cleddau shows how trade has always been an important feature of the settlement, Haverfordwest having grown up around the lowest fording point and the highest point of navigation on the river. Ships of up to 200 tons could reach the quays and in the 13th and 14th century the port was most important in the trade of wool and hides. Corn and general goods were still being shipped from the port until 1853 when the coming of the railway led to its demise.

In 1200 Robert of Hwlffordd founded an Augustinian Priory, the ruins of which can still be seen on the river bank downstream of the Old Quay. After its abandonment, some artefacts, such as the carved bench ends of the mayoral pew, were transferred to St Mary's Church at the top of the High Street. One of the most interesting churches in the county, and arguably in Wales as a whole, St Mary's has some excellent architectural features and carvings. However, it has little to show that it is in Wales, and not England, as the only Welsh features of the church are an ape playing a harp and a pig playing a *crwth*.

Picton Castle is an ancient building, though so greatly altered into a residential property as to leave little of the defensive structure visible. It has been, and still is, occupied by one family, the descendants of the original founders who came to the area in the 13th century. The house is occasionally open to the public (an admission charge is levied) and the surroundings are most pleasant to visit at any time of the year, and the 40 acres of grounds and gardens are a must for anyone remotely interested in horticulture and beautiful plants and trees of all sorts.

Llawhaden village is worthy of exploration and the inquisitive traveller is well-rewarded, even if visiting the church does involve a steep descent and tough climb back. There are superb views from the castle, which is worth a prolonged visit. It was built to protect the possessions of the bishops of St Davids. The village was established at the same time as the Norman castle, whilst the church, that gives the village its name (Llawhaden: the church of Aidan), was built in the 14th century on an older site and incorporates an early Christian monument in the east wall. Although the church was rebuilt in the 19th century, it is still very attractive and has a fine crenellated tower. The village was revived in the 16th century by the Skyrme family, and in the 17th century was a hotbed of nonconformity. Today it is a sleepy settlement that makes an ideal base for exploring Llawhaden parish, noted for its high concentration of prehistoric and historic sites, and the beautiful Eastern Cleddau valley.

Wiston is another castle site and takes its name from the man who built the original motte and bailey in the 12th century, on the site of a prehistoric settlement. He rejoiced in the name of Wizo the Fleming! Later additions and rebuilding did not stop the Welsh capturing the site in 1147 and 1193 and finally destroying it in 1220, when a new site (Picton) was chosen by the then displaced lord. The castle is a well-preserved example of a motte and bailey.

In addition to some superb views *en route*, the wildlife is extensive and varied, the wild flowers alone being a good reason to cycle this route in spring.

As Haverfordwest is surrounded on all sides by a non-cyclist-friendly ring of busy roads—multi-lane in places—and the centre is a maze of one-way systems and pedestrian precincts, parts of the recommended route through the town involve dismounting and walking, as well as negotiating some potentially awkward, if short, flights of steps. If you do not fancy this, you can either brave the traffic or avoid the steps by choosing your own route through the town to avoid the riverside.

Route

1. From the castle entrance, descend Castle Street towards the churchyard. Turn right down North Street and follow the one-way system down Holloway to a mini-roundabout. Go across the roundabout, dismount and cross the Old Bridge, then turn right and head through the pedestrian Riverside Quay shopping area. At the clock tower by the footbridge, go straight along the Riverside down the side of Boots Chemist and up onto the end of the bridge. Between the clock tower and Picton Place, at the end of the bridge, you will have to negotiate some short flights of steps.

2. On reaching the road at the top of the steps leading to Picton Place, turn left and walk down to a busy roundabout. Leave the roundabout via the exit opposite, signposted to Uzmaston.

   If you prefer to stay on your bike and risk the traffic from the mini-roundabout at the bottom of Holloway, turn left and at the major roundabout ahead, turn right. At the next roundabout, turn right again and follow the dual carriageway to a third major roundabout. Exit on the minor road signposted to Uzmaston.

3. Follow the minor road for about ¾ mile, through suburban housing, to a T-junction with Creamston Road. Turn left and follow the lane signposted to Rhos. Ignoring side turns, you will come to a crossroads within the space of about one mile.

4. Turn right at the crossroads and follow a rolling, single-track lane, signposted to Millin, for about 1¼ miles. Cross Millin Brook and at the T-junction ahead, turn right. This lane eventually brings you to a T-junction, where you can *either* turn right (a dead end) to admire the view across the confluence of the Eastern and Western Cleddau—the two rivers joining to become the Daugleddau—*or* turn left and

follow the main route, through woodland and past the entrance to Picton Castle, to a T-junction at Rhos.

5. Turn left at the junction and follow the lane, ignoring all side turns, as far as the A40.

6. At the A40, turn left, then immediately right, signposted to Wiston. Follow this lane for about 3 miles, ignoring side turns, to a T-junction where you turn left, signposted to Llawhaden and Llys-y-frân. Follow the road for about 2½ miles until you come to a T-junction near the village of Llawhaden.

7. Turn right to explore the attractive and historic village, or turn left, signposted to Gelli, to continue on the main route.

8. About half a mile north-west of Llawhaden you descend to Plain Dealings, where you take the second left turn, signposted Unsuitable for Long Vehicles. This lane, which heads past Llawhaden Community Playing Field and a telephone box, provides a superb downhill run to Cotland Mill bridge. Beyond the bridge, climb sharply up to a T-junction.

9. Turn left at the T-junction, signposted to Wiston, and follow the lane for about 2 miles on its climb up to the village. At the T-junction on the fringes of Wiston, turn left and then turn right at a second T-junction, signposted to Wiston, despite having passed the Wiston village sign! Beware of ducks!

10. Follow the lane for some 4 miles, first passing Wiston Church and Castle (both worth a visit), before enjoying a long downhill run as far as the railway line and Cartlett Brook. After crossing the valley bottom, climb to a T-junction in Crundale.

11. Turn left at the junction and at the next T-junction, where the route joins the B4329 by the General Picton pub, turn left again. Follow the B4329 to a roundabout. Head straight over and on to a T-junction in Prendergast, opposite a floor-covering centre.

12. Turn left at the junction. This brings you down to a busy roundabout on the fringe of Haverfordwest town centre. My advice is to dismount and follow the pedestrian underpass to the town centre by the Riverside Quay shopping area, before retracing your steps up to the start.

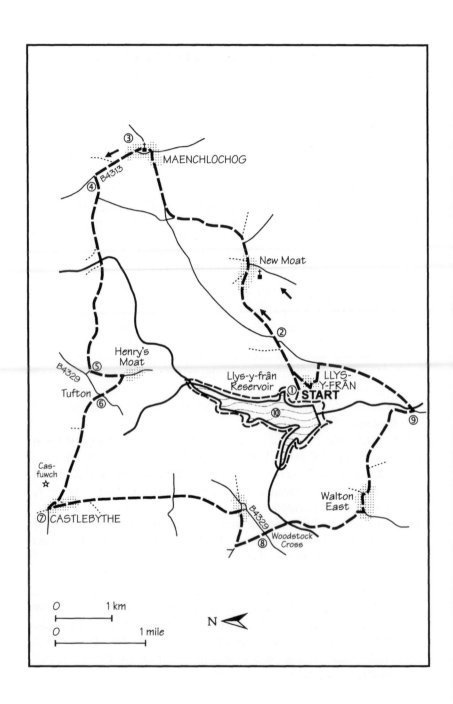

MAENCHLOCHOG

New Moat

Llys-y-frân
Reservoir

LLYS-
Y-FRÂN
START

Henry's
Moat

B4329

Tufton

Cas-
fuwch
☆

CASTLEBYTHE

Walton
East

Woodstock
Cross

B4329

B4313

0   1 km

0   1 mile

N

20 Llys-y-Frân, Maenclochog and Castlebythe

Fact File

Distance:	17 miles (27.3 km) or 24½ miles (39.4 km)
Time:	4-6 hours
Maps:	OS Landranger 145 Cardigan & Mynydd Preseli; OS Outdoor Leisure 35 North Pembrokeshire
Start:	Llys-y-frân car park SN 041245
Terrain:	Mainly quiet lanes and minor roads. The optional Llys-y-frân circuit is on a good track but steep and muddy in places.
Refreshments:	Cafe/restaurant and gift shop at start Maenclochog: Globe Inn and shops Tufton: Tufton Arms
Parking:	See Start
Suitable for:	Most cyclists
Cycle Hire:	At Llys-y-frân Country Park.

Along the way

For a description of Maenclochog and sites within vicinity, see Ride 12: Rosebush and Gors Fawr, p. 73.

Most of the villages you pass through on this ride have some kind of earthworks within their bounds or nearby; Henry's Moat and Castlebythe both boast mottes; Walton East, an early settlement and homestead; while on the flanks of Mynydd Castlebythe is Cas-fuwch. Cairns, standing stones and other earthworks also dot the area.

Llys-y-frân is best known for its reservoir and Country Park, opened in 1972 by HRH Princess Margaret. Initially built to serve the Milford Haven oil terminals and refineries, the 187 acre lake was formed by impounding the waters of Afon Syfynwy behind a 100ft concrete dam. However, unless you are right beside it, the dam, now a popular attraction, does not intrude on the scene.

Around the reservoir is a well-graded perimeter track which may be used by walkers and cyclists. The track replaces a waterside path (as marked on the maps) that became unusable when the water level was raised in the mid 1990s. The path passes through a nature reserve and conservation area: sessile oakwoods provide breeding sites for sparrow-hawk, buzzards, woodpeckers, jays and nuthatches, while goldcrests nest in the sitka spruce plantations. The reservoir attracts a multitude of water fowl, while mammals in the area include foxes, badgers and squirrels. The Country Park is a haven for those interested in fishing, bird-watching, canoeing, kayaking, sailing, boardsailing, and—occasionally—abseiling down the dam wall.

Llys-y-frân translates as 'court of crows' but there is little to suggest that members of the crow family are more numerous here than elsewhere in the vicinity.

Route

1. From Llys-y-frân Country Park car park, head back along the access road, keeping straight on at the T-junction and ignoring the lane that leads to Llys-y-frân village. At the next T-junction follow the signs to Maenclochog.
2. At the next T-junction, about 450 yards ahead, turn right, signposted to New Moat. About one mile ahead, at the T-junction in the village, head straight on to the centre of Maenclochog, a journey of some 2 miles.
3. Continue northwards through the village, past the church, to a T-junction about ¾ mile beyond the church.
4. Turn left and follow the lane, signposted to Tufton, up and down hill for some 2¼ miles.
5. Some 50 yards before reaching the T-junction with the often busy B4329, turn left at a minor T-junction and head south towards Henry's Moat. At the next T-junction, at the northern end of the hamlet, turn right and ride up to the crossroads in Tufton.
6. Go straight across the B4329 and follow the quiet lane that leads to Castlebythe, signposted to Puncheston.

7. At the crossroads in Castlebythe, near the tree-covered mound or motte, turn left and follow the lane almost due south for about 2 miles, following signs to Walton East. At the second of two crossroads (just short of the main B4329), turn right. At a T-junction half a mile ahead, turn left, signposted to Woodstock Cross and Clarbeston Road and follow the minor road to Woodstock Cross.

8. At Woodstock Cross, head carefully across the B4329 and continue along the lane, signposted to Clarbeston Road and Walton East, past an ancient fort, to a T-junction a little beyond the Walton East village sign. Turn left and head through the main part of the hamlet, with its attractive church, green and duckpond. Follow the winding lane, which descends past another ancient enclosure, to a T-junction at the bottom of the Syfynwy valley.

9. Turn left, head over the bridge, signposted to Llys-y-frân, New Moat and Maenclochog, and climb a distance of about 1 mile to a T-junction on the ridge overlooking Llys-y-frân. Turn left at the junction and head down the slope above Llys-y-frân to a T-junction where you rejoin the access road to the Country Park. Turn left and return to the car park at the start of the ride.

10. Those with energy to spare may wish to follow the 7 mile track around the reservoir. The trackway, which starts and finishes by the shop, is clear and easy to follow. A small charge is payable at the shop for this section.

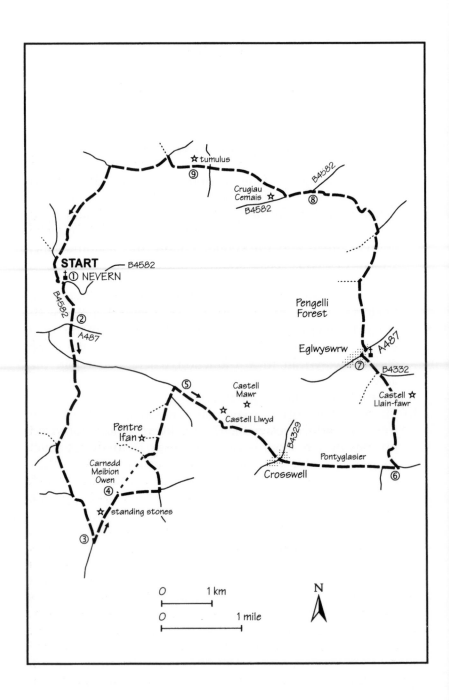

21 Nevern and Pentre Ifan

Fact File

Distance:	17 miles (27.3 km)
Time:	4-5 hours
Maps:	OS Landranger 145 Cardigan & Mynydd Preseli; OS Outdoor Leisure 35 North Pembrokeshire
Start:	Nevern church SN 083400
Terrain:	Mainly quiet lanes and minor roads. Some steep climbs and descents. An optional half mile off-road section of green lane riding.
Refreshments:	Nevern: Trewern Arms Eglwyswrw: Butchers Arms and small shop
Parking:	Limited roadside parking at Start
Suitable for:	The family fit enough to cope with the numerous hills. Take care when crossing the A487, a busy road with poor visibility at the crossing points.

Along the way

This route takes in some splendid scenery, through a part of Pembrokeshire that is steeped in legend and dotted with prehistoric and early Christian monuments. For a description of the stones outside and inside Nevern church, the church itself, Nevern castle and the legends associated with the area, see Ride 5: St Dogmaels and Nevern, p. 27.

Pentre Ifan cromlech is probably one of the most well-known, megalithic monuments in Wales. Magnificently sited on a ridge overlooking the Nyfer valley and within view of Carn Ingli and its hill-top fort, Pentre Ifan burial chamber was constructed by Neolithic people about 5,500 years ago. It was originally covered with an earthen mound, now eroded away, which was aligned approximately north-south. It rose about 12ft above the southern end of the cromlech, where the chamber and its curved portal of standing stones were set. Today Pentre Ifan consists of three main upright supports on which rest the massive capstone. The capstone, measuring about 17′ x 10′ and weighing around 16 tons, stands some 7′ 6″ above the floor of the burial chamber and is an impressive sight.

In addition to the Iron Age hill-fort on the summit of Carn Ingli, other forts glimpsed *en route* include Castell Llwyd, Castell Mawr and Castell Llain-fawr, as well as a motte and bailey a little off-route in Eglwyswrw. Near Eglwyswrw lies the beautiful Pengelli Forest, now a haven for wildlife but once a busy area of timber production for industrial purposes.

North of Eglwyswrw, on the high ground overlooking Nant Duad is Crugiau Cemais, now a viewpoint but known to archaeologists as the site of three Bronze Age cairns.

Route

1. From the church at Nevern, head south over the bridge, past the Trewern Arms, and up to the crossroads at Temple Bar.
2. Take great care as you cross the A487 and follow the lane opposite, signposted to Cilgwyn and Cwm Gwaun, and as Unsuitable for Coaches. Go straight over the next crossroads, again following signs to Cilgwyn and Cwm Gwaun. *En route* to the first T-junction the road dips and climbs. At the T-junction, turn left and bear left at the second, both on uphill sections.
3. At the next T-junction at the top of the ridge, turn left. Several standing stones may be seen in the fields either side of the road as you gently descend the eastern flank of the ridge.
4. Where the lane turns sharp right, as you approach the dramatic rock outcrops of Carnedd Meibion Owen, you have the option of *either* going straight on along a green lane—a bridleway which is rough but fun—*or* staying on surfaced lanes for a longer downhill, easy ride. If you opt to follow the road, head down to the crossroads and turn left, to rejoin the 'rough riders' on a bend by the entrance drive to Tycanol. Continue down the lane, past the entrance to

Pentre Ifan (a visit is highly recommended and you can wheel your bike right into the site for safety), straight on at the first minor T-junction by the stables and then right at the next, more major, T-junction.

5. Follow the minor road for some 3 miles up the Nyfer valley, ignoring all side turns. Head straight across the B4329 at the crossroads in Crosswell and follow signs to Crymych. At a T-junction by an attractive stone-built cottage, a short distance beyond Pontyglasier, turn left to follow a lane signposted as Unsuitable for Long Vehicles.

6. The lane crosses the Afon Nyfer before climbing up to the B4332. Bear left and follow the road to Eglwyswrw, where the B4332 meets the A487.

7. At the T-junction by the church, turn right, signposted to Cardigan, then take the next left turn just beyond the village Post Office and shop. Ignoring side turns, follow the road as far as Trewilym. At the farm, turn right at the first T-junction and then left at the next. Follow the road as it descends the southern slopes of the Duad valley, over the bridge across Nant Duad and up the northern slopes as far as a T-junction.

8. At the junction, bear left and follow the B4582 for some 650 yards to the junction below Crugiau Cemais. Turn right and follow the road signposted to Newport Beach. (The entrance to Crugiau Cemais viewpoint is situated a short distance beyond the junction.)

9. Follow the lane, going straight over the crossroads about a mile ahead, signposted to Newport Beach. At the next two T-junctions, turn left (the first signposted to Newport Beach, the second to Nevern). On approaching Nevern, at journey's end, the road steepens as it heads past the site of Nevern castle.

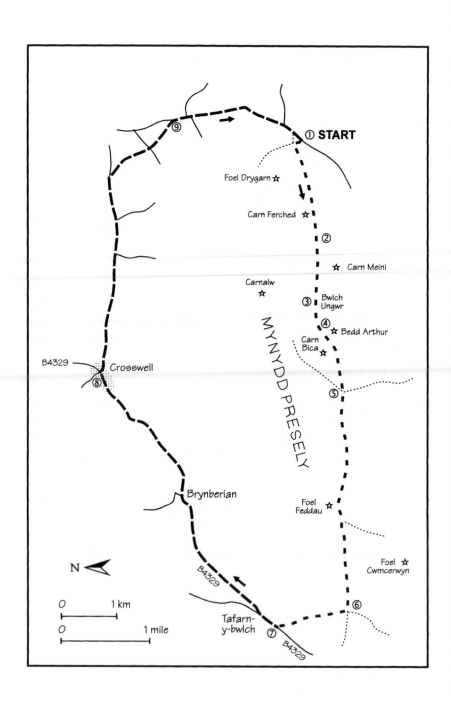

Foel Drygarn ☆

Carn Ferched ☆

②

☆ Carn Meini

Carnalw
☆

③ Bwlch
Ungwr

④ ☆ Bedd Arthur

Carn
Bica ☆

⑤

MYNYDD PRESELY

① START

⑨

B4329 Crosswell
⑧

Brynberian

Foel
Feddau ☆

Foel ☆
Cwmcerwyn

N ◀

O   1 km

O   1 mile

⑥

Tafarn-
y-bwlch
⑦ B4329

B4329

22 The Presely Hills Ridge

Fact File

Distance:	14 miles (22.5 km)
Time:	4-6 hours, depending on your fitness
Maps:	OS Landranger 145 Cardigan & Mynydd Preseli; OS Pathfinder 1033 Newport (Trefdraeth) & Eglwyswrw; OS Outdoor Leisure 35 North Pembrokeshire
Start:	Roadside parking at SN 165330
Terrain:	Hill tracks and mainly quiet roads and lanes. The hills can be wet and muddy. To avoid excessive erosion, please do this ride only in dry weather, when your tyres will do less damage.
Refreshments:	None
Parking:	See Start
Suitable for:	Mountain biking for the fit!

PLEASE NOTE

Prevent Skids—ride with control to prevent erosion, especially in wet conditions.

Stay on the Trail—do not ride off the trail.

Be Courteous and Considerate—always give way to walkers and riders even if it means dismounting.

Be Safe: take Food, Whistle and Compass; wear a Helmet and carry Waterproofs and Spare Clothing—weather conditions on the Presely Hills can be very changeable.

Livestock—do not startle or disturb livestock, and respect the life of the countryside.

Along the way

Half of this 14 mile ride is on the open hill, whilst the other half follows fairly quiet roads and lanes, and passes many sites of prehistoric and historic interest. The first 5 miles can prove quite hard work as you climb on hill tracks, but the views make it all worthwhile. As some of the hill tracks are

147

Garn Gŵr, Foel Drygarn (Ride 22).

Ruins of St Teilo's Church, Llandeilo (Ride 23).

quite soft, and very soft in wet weather, I advise anyone contemplating the ride to undertake it during the summer when drier weather will help prevent too much environmental damage being caused by tyres.

For a description of that part of the route between the start and Carn Bica, and points of interest relating to Foel Cwmcerwyn, see Ride 13: The Golden Road and Rhos-fach, p. 81.

Between Carn Bica and the summit of Foel Feddau, topped, as the name suggests, by Bronze Age burial cairns, are Cerrig y Marchogion, a row of small tors. West of Foel Feddau the route heads down the rough and in places, boggy hillside, to join B4329 near Tafarn-y-bwlch, south-west of Brynberian. After leaving the grass and mud for tarmac, you can enjoy some good downhill free-wheeling on the occasionally busy B4329, and then some more level cycling along quiet lanes in the Nyfer and Bannon valley, before a final stiff climb up to the end of the ride, and your car.

This route can also be ridden in the opposite direction: the harder climbs would then be on surfaced roads and the prevailing wind would be on your back across the hills. I prefer the clockwise option but the hill section is arguably harder this way round.

Route

1-4. For a description of the first part of the route (1-4), as far as the col west of Carn Bica, see Ride 13, p. 86.

5. On the floor of the boggy col beyond Carn Bica, the ridge is crossed by a faint north-south track. Go straight on, following the faint path that heads past Cerrig y Marchogion, over Foel Feddau and down the northern boundary fence of the forestry plantation to the track junction at Bwlch Pennant.

6. At this rather boggy col, turn right and head north, away from the gate in the forestry fence, on what was the old carriage road, now replaced by the B4329. Although faint at first, the track becomes more obvious (and drier) as you

descend.

7. On reaching the road, turn right and follow the B4329 for some 3¼ miles past Brynberian (the road bypasses the village) to Crosswell.

8. Turn right at the old pump alongside the crossroads at Crosswell, signposted to Crymych. Follow the lane east for some 2¼ miles, ignoring side turns, to a T-junction, where you bear right to continue along the 'main' road. Go straight across a crossroads and, following the signs to Crymych, on to a T-junction, less than half a mile from the crossroads.

9. Bear right at the junction and at the next T-junction, on a bend, head straight on, signposted to 3 C's Caravans. Follow this lane uphill—steep in places—for some 1¼ miles, ignoring side turns, to a T-junction. Bear right, signposted to Mynachlog-ddu and Maenclochog, and continue to the start of the ride which lies a short distance ahead.

The moon rises over Llys-y-Frân (Ride 20).

The pilgrims' cross at Nevern (Ride 21).

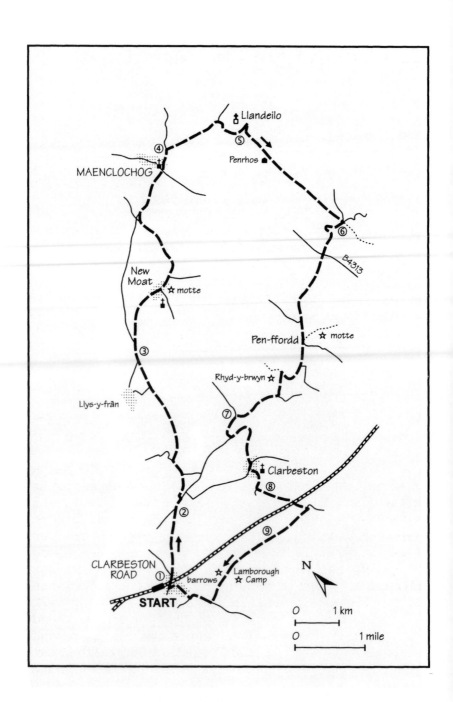

23 Clarbeston Road and Maenclochog

Fact File

Distance:	18 miles (28.9 km)
Time:	4½ to 5½ hours
Maps:	OS Landranger 158 Tenby & surrounding area; OS Outdoor Leisure 35 North Pembrokeshire and 36 South Pembrokeshire
Start:	Clarbeston Road SN 015209
Terrain:	Mainly quiet lanes through rolling country-side. Some steep climbs and descents.
Refreshments:	Maenclochog: Globe Inn and shops Clarbeston Road: Cross Inn and Picton Inn, and PO stores
Parking:	Roadside in village
Suitable for:	Fitter cyclists who enjoy rolling countryside, with some steep climbs.

Along the way

For details relating to Maenclochog and sites in the vicinity, and information about St Teilo's Church, Llandeilo, see Ride 12: Rosebush and Gors Fawr, p. 73.

Until the arrival of Brunel's railway in 1853, Clarbeston Road was a hamlet known as New Cross. But with the opening of the railway station, its fortunes changed dramatically and it grew to be a centre of trade and business for local farmers. Although those busy days are long since passed, Clarbeston Road station, so-named by Brunel, remains as does the road bridge, also a Brunel creation. The village is now a quiet spot, except when trains rattle through on their way to and from Milford Haven, Fishguard and the towns and cities to the east.

South-east of Clarbeston Road, two Bronze Age round barrows lie in a roadside field, known as Corner Piece, and nearby is a small Iron Age hill-fort called Lamborough Camp. New Moat, a planned Norman settlement of the 12th century,

The Green Bridge of Wales, Castlemartin (Ride 26).

Camrose mill (Ride 27).

has a motte and bailey and a Norman church tower, and, nearby, the remains of a medieval field system.

A short distance east of Pen-ffordd stands a medieval motte, whilst to the west is a fine example of an inland promontory fort called Rhyd-y-brwyn.

St Martin of Tour's Church in Clarbeston is a handsome village church, medieval in origin, though renovated in Victorian times, with a battlemented square tower. Standing on the Pilgrims' Route from Llawhaden to St Davids, the church was once of great importance and was presented to the Knights of St John, at Slebech Commandery, in the 12th century by the family of Wizo the Fleming, the powerful lord whose power base was nearby Wiston.

Route

1. From Clarbeston Road, head north-east over the railway crossing, signposted to Llys-y-frân, New Moat and Maenclochog. Stay on this road for approximately 1¼ miles: at the second T-junction, a short way beyond the first, turn left, signposted to Llys-y-frân Country Park.
2. Continue along this lane for the next 2 miles until you come to a T-junction where you turn right, signposted to Maenclochog.
3. At the next T-junction, about 450 yards ahead, turn right, signposted to New Moat, and follow the road through the hamlet to Maenclochog. At the centre of Maenclochog turn right by the church and head along the road between the shop and garage, signposted to Mynachlog-ddu, Crymych, Llangolman and Rhos-fach.
4. About a quarter of a mile ahead, after crossing a bridge, turn right, signposted to Llangolman. Follow this lane to a T-junction where you turn right, signposted to Llanycefn. St Teilo's church ruins are to be found behind the first farm on your left along the lane. To visit the church, leave your bike and walk through the gateway between the barns, follow a track by the end of the house and through a gate;

turn right at the wall to enter the ruinous churchyard via a rickety gate.

5. After retracing your steps from the church, follow the lane —which climbs steeply out of the valley south of Llandeilo— for the next 2½ miles, passing Pen-rhos, the last traditionally thatched cottage in Pembrokeshire, as far as a crossroads where you turn right, signposted to Llan-y-cefn.

6. Continue along this road as it drops and climbs steeply to a crossroads with the B4313. Go straight on and follow the narrow lane, signposted to Pen-ffordd. Head along the lane for the next 3½ miles, ignoring all side turns, as it dips, climbs and winds its way through glorious countryside.

7. At a T-junction above the floor of the Syfynwy valley, turn left, signposted to Clarbeston Road. A little further ahead, beyond the bridge across Afon Syfynwy, turn left at a T-junction, signposted to Clarbeston. At the first T-junction in Clarbeston village, turn right, signposted to Clarbeston Road. At the second, turn left, signposted to Llawhaden and as Unsuitable for HGVs.

8. South of Clarbeston, the road heads over a railway bridge, beyond which lies a T-junction beside a bridge over a stream. Turn right at the T-junction.

9. Follow the lane (perhaps an ancient ridge route) to a T-junction some 2¼ miles ahead. Turn right to regain the start of the ride in Clarbeston Road.

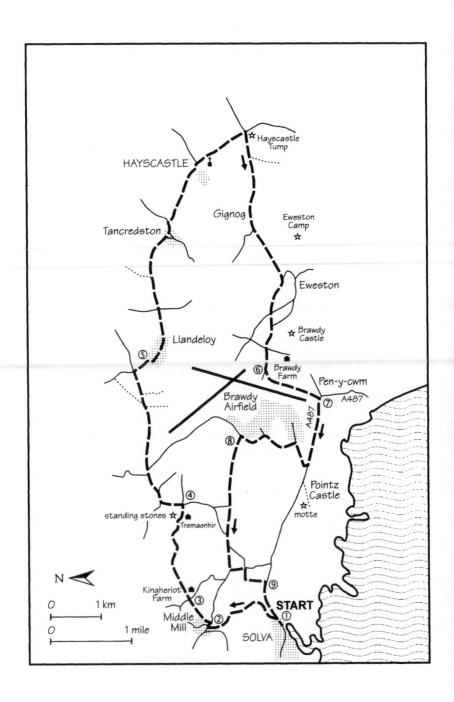

24 Solva and Hayscastle

Fact File

Distance:	19 miles (30.5 km)
Time:	4½ to 5½ hours
Maps:	OS Landranger 157 St Davids & Haverfordwest; OS Outdoor Leisure 35 North Pembrokeshire
Start:	Solva car park SN 806242
Nearest Town:	St Davids
Terrain:	Mainly quiet lanes. Fairly level but with a couple of short, sharp dips and climbs.
Refreshments:	Solva: everything available Middle Mill: woollen mill and cafe
Parking:	See Start
Suitable for:	Most cyclists, but there are some short sections of busy main road. Younger cyclists should be closely supervised on these sections.

Along the way

Solva has one of the best natural harbours in Pembrokeshire and, not surprisingly, this has been the reason for its development over the ages. Prehistoric and historic remains litter the area: east of the village lies St Elvis burial chamber of Neolithic age whilst on the Gribin, the ridge overlooking the harbour, are the defences of an Iron Age promontory fort.

The harbour, despite its narrow entrance, was used by both fishing and trading vessels. Limestone was imported in great quantity to be burnt in the impressive row of limekilns to be seen from the car park. Limestone was burnt in order to produce lime, used both as a fertiliser and for building purposes. The village, which grew up around the harbour and developed rapidly in the 18th century, has many historical buildings, including the inn and the parish church.

An interesting, but thankfully discontinued local custom was the tradition of hauling a corpse feet-first up the chimney

161

of the house within which it had been lying. This ceremony, performed at midnight on the night before the funeral, was supposed to help the soul on its journey up to heaven!

Middle Mill—or Felinganol—has an early 20th-century flannel and cloth mill which, unlike most, has remained in production. Solva Woollen Mill, now a tourist attraction and well worth a visit, specialises in the manufacture of carpets and floor rugs.

The nearby Baptist chapel was first established in 1756. John Reynolds, who served as minister of this chapel in 1794, was said to have been a traitor, in sympathy with the French during their 'invasion' of Pembrokeshire at Carreg Wastad in 1797. His home was raided, papers taken and the effigy of his friend Henry Davies, minister of Llangloffan, was burnt in Fishguard Fair. However, the accusations were proved false, though I find no record of any apology being made to him!

At Tremaenhir the two standing stones—one very shapely —on the opposite side of the road to the farmhouse are clearly visible. A third stone is said to have been used in building part of the house. Other prehistoric sites along the route include: Eweston Camp, an Iron Age fort overlooking Brawdy Brook; Brawdy Castle, an inland promontory fort to the east of Brawdy Farm; and Hayscastle Tump, a possible Bronze Age round barrow, situated by the roadside at a crossroads west of Hayscastle Cross.

More recent historical sites include Pointz Castle, a 12th-century medieval earthwork castle about 1½ miles east of Solva, and Hayscastle motte. Hayscastle itself was one of the communities planned by the Norman invaders and probably founded in the 12th century. A 'lost' village lies under part of Hayscastle Farm but today only the small Celtic-style church, restored in the 19th century, and the wooded motte are visible reminders that this was once an important site.

Brawdy Airfield, once an RAF base and home to search and rescue helicopters, is now an army base.

This ride is rich in history and covers a part of Pembrokeshire that deserves greater exploration.

Route

1. From the car park, turn right and follow the road through the village, past shops, pubs and a gallery, to a T-junction by the Cambrian Inn. Instead of following the A487 over the bridge, turn left, signposted to Tre-groes/Whitchurch and Middle Mill. Follow the road up the valley of the River Solva, past some very attractive houses, as far as a T-junction about one mile north of Solva. Turn right over the bridge, signposted to Llandeloy. Entry to Solva Woollen Mill, at Middle Mill, is free of charge.
2. After crossing the bridge, bear right then steeply left at a T-junction a few yards ahead. This narrow, grass-grown lane climbs and zigzags its way to a crossroads at Kingheriot Farm.
3. Go straight over the crossroads and follow the lane to a second crossroads beyond Tremaenhir, noted for its standing stones.
4. Turn left at the crossroads, signposted to Croes-goch. Ignoring all side turns, follow the minor road, signposted to Llandeloy, for the next two miles to a crossroads. Turn right and follow the signs to Llandeloy.
5. Continue through the pleasant hamlet of Llandeloy to the next crossroads. Head straight on, signposted to Hayscastle and Tancredston. Ignoring side turns, continue along the lane for some 3 miles, through Tancredston, then right at a T-junction at Hayscastle and on to the crossroads at Hayscastle Tump, now hidden by trees. Turn right at the crossroads, signposted (almost invisibly) to Brawdy and Llandeloy.
6. Follow this winding lane for the next 3½ miles or so, ignoring side turns, until you come to a T-junction a short distance north of Brawdy Farm. Turn left, signposted to Pen-y-cwm. In about 1 mile the road joins the A487. Turn right at the T-junction, signposted to St Davids and Solva.
7. Follow the A487 for approximately 1 mile, before turning right at the first T-junction, signposted 14th Signal Regiment. At the next T-junction, by the Business Park, turn

left, signposted to a camp and caravan site. Follow the lane for about ¾ mile to a T-junction just past the Caravan Park.

8. Turn left at the T-junction. As you head in a westerly direction along the lane, go straight on at the first T-junction; left at the second, signposted to Solva and Middle Mill; straight on at the third, signposted to Middle Mill; and left at the fourth. This brings you to a crossroads where you turn right, signposted to Solva.

9. After about half a mile you rejoin the A487. At the T-junction, turn right, signposted to St Davids, and drop back down into Solva and the start of the ride.

Tremaenhir (Ride 24).

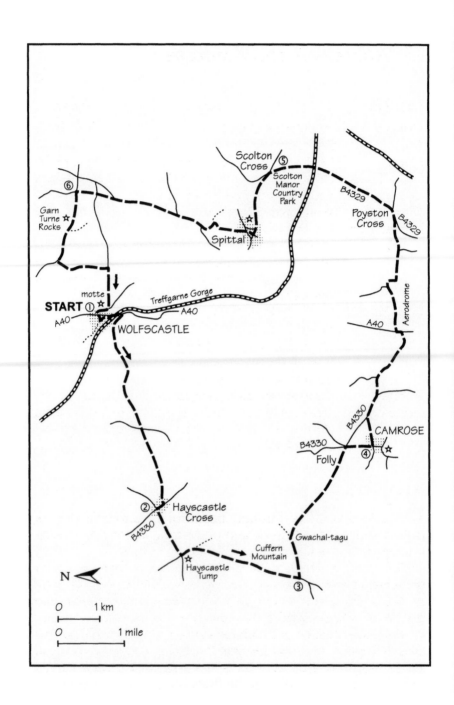

25 Wolfscastle and Camrose

Fact File

Distance:	22 miles (35.3 km)
Time:	5-6 hours
Maps:	OS Landranger 157 St Davids & Haverfordwest; OS Outdoor Leisure 35 North Pembrokeshire and 36 South Pembrokeshire
Start:	Wolfscastle SM 956266
Nearest Town:	Haverfordwest
Terrain:	Mainly quiet lanes and minor roads through flat and gently rolling countryside. The section on the B4329 can be busy, as can the crossing of the A40.
Refreshments:	Wolfscastle: Country Hotel, PO shop and New Wolfe Inn
	Hayscastle Cross: Cross Inn
	Spittal: shop and pub
	Scolton Manor tearooms
Parking:	Limited roadside parking in Wolfscastle
Suitable for:	Most cyclists, though younger riders should be closely supervised when crossing the A40 and on the B4329.

Along the way

This ride takes you through beautiful countryside that is dotted with sites of historic and prehistoric interest, as well as offering fine views and a great variety of wild life.

Wolfscastle is medieval in origin: it is one of many Norman settlements founded to consolidate their holdings in this part of Wales. The green is thought to have been at the centre of the medieval village, whilst the 12th-century motte and bailey castle, one of a chain of Landsker forts, is now cut off from the main village by the road. Despite the village's Norman origins, Wolfscastle may well have been in existence at a much earlier date. There is no evidence to support the stories that the

Romans mined gold in the area, but Roman remains have been found at nearby Ford and Upper Newton Farm. Near Ford Camp, an Iron Age fort, Roman tiles and bricks were found, which were said to belong to a bath house.

Another possible Iron Age fort is to be found in Spittal. The village boasts a 13th-century church containing an inscribed stone from the 5th-6th century. The translated Latin inscription reads '(the stone) of Evalus, son of Dencuus. Cuniovende, his mother (erected it)'. The village takes its name from St Mary's Hospitium, built about 1290 but which was finally demolished in the 19th century. There is also a holy well, the Lady Well, near the churchyard. St Mary's stood on the pilgrim route from Llawhaden to St Davids and was a possession of the Bishop of St Davids.

North-west of Spittal is Treffgarne Gorge, overlooked by a spectacular Iron Age hill-fort. Within the gorge are the remains of Brunel's broad-gauge railway line, a failed venture. The present line was opened in 1906.

Treffgarne and Plumstone Mountains are noted for their imposing crags of ancient volcanic rocks which rise above the moorland, dominating the area and its prehistoric remains. The latter include an Iron Age fort and possible remains of a Neolithic chambered tomb. Other chambered tombs are to be found a few miles north of Spittal, near Garn Turne Rocks and Parc-y-Llyn.

For those with a gruesome turn of mind, gallows once stood at Scolton Cross, just north of Scolton Manor Country Park and museum (well worth a visit). The cross was once known as Gallows Cross.

Although some Stone Age artefacts have come to light in the village, Camrose is a Norman settlement but the motte and bailey castle has been eroded by cultivation. Medieval field patterns have been identified north of the village. Once important for its fulling and woollen mill (Anne Boleyn was at one time the owner of Camrose mill), Camrose is now a quiet spot bypassed by the B4330. The village church, dedicated to St Ishmael, has an interesting tower, and anyone interested in architecture should make time for a visit.

Intriguing place-names are also encountered on this ride: you will pass near the ruins of Step Inn, near Start Naked, and Gwachal-tagu, which roughly translated means 'beware of choking'.

Route

1. From the A40 near the village green, take the minor road by the side of the Wolfscastle Country Hotel and follow it as it zigzags down, past a garden with the most amazing water features, to a T-junction beneath the road bridge that carries the A40. Turn right, signposted to Haverfordwest, cross the old bridge, and follow the road up to the A40. Turn right and then, almost immediately, right again by the New Wolfe Inn, leaving the busy A40 for a minor road, signposted to Hayscastle. If the A40 is very busy, I would recommend you push your bike from junction to junction to avoid crossing and recrossing the road.

   Ignoring side turns, follow the minor road for some 3 miles to a T-junction in Hayscastle Cross. Turn right, signposted to Roch.

2. At the crossroads in the centre of the village, by the Cross Inn, turn left, again signposted to Roch. Follow the minor road to another crossroads at Hayscastle Tump, a Bronze Age burial mound now almost lost in the undergrowth. Turn left at the crossroads, signposted to Roch. Follow the road across the flank of Cuffern Mountain, as far as the second T-junction, a distance of some two miles.

3. Turn left, signposted to Camrose, and follow the road for approximately 2½ miles, passing Gwachal-tagu within the space of about half a mile.

   At Folly, at the end of the 2½ mile stretch of road, is a 5-road junction. Turn right, signposted Camrose. The centre of the village lies half a mile ahead.

4. Turn left in the centre of Camrose and, on reaching the B4330, turn right towards Haverfordwest. About a third of a mile further on, turn left and follow a minor road,

signposted to Fishguard and Haverfordwest, which leads down across the Western Cleddau and up to the A40. At the A40, turn left, towards Fishguard, then immediately right in order to follow a minor road, signposted to Clarbeston Road, that runs along the northern boundary of Haverfordwest Aerodrome. Stay on this road, ignoring side turnings, until you come to Poyston Cross. Turn left and head north along the occasionally very busy B4329. Beware of the traffic!

5. Some 2¼ miles north of Poyston Cross, beyond the entrance to Scolton Manor Country Park, lies Scolton Cross crossroads. Turn left, signposted to Spittal, and continue down to the crossroads just beyond the church in Spittal. Turn right and head past the unfenced play area to a T-junction/staggered crossroads. Go straight across and follow a minor lane that leads roughly northwards. After about ¾ mile of winding lane, you come to a T-junction where you turn right. Head across the bridge over Spittal Brook (lovely name!) and continue for some 1½ miles to a T-junction where you turn left, signposted to Little Newcastle. Go straight across the first crossroads, signposted to Little Newcastle, and on past a nursing home to the next crossroads.

6. Turn left, signposted to Letterston, and descend past Garn Turne Rocks and burial chamber to a T-junction some 1¼ miles from the crossroads. At the T-junction, turn left and follow the lane for about a mile to another T-junction. Turn right and head towards Wolfscastle, passing beneath the motte and bailey and under the A40. Beyond the road bridge, turn right to climb back to the start of the ride.

A wise sculpture! Scolton Manor Country Park (Ride 25).

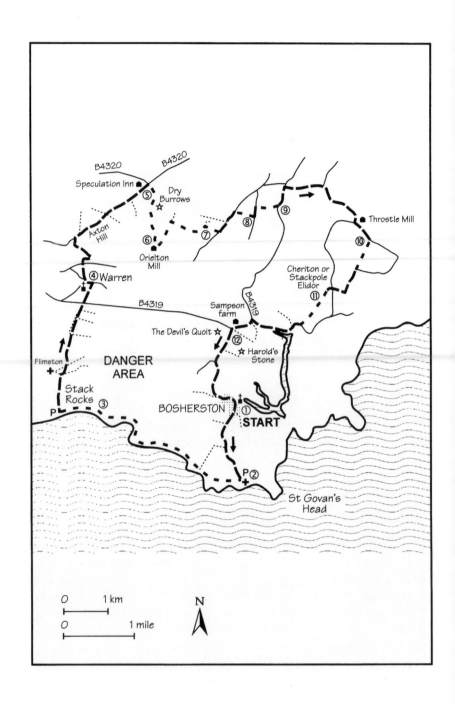

B4320

B4320

Speculation Inn

⑤

Dry Burrows

Axton Hill

⑥

Orielton Mill

⑦

⑧

⑨

Throstle Mill

⑩

④ Warren

B4319

Cheriton or Stackpole Elidor

⑪

Flimston

Sampson farm

B4319

The Devil's Quoit ☆

⑫

Harold's Stone

DANGER AREA

Stack Rocks

P ③

BOSHERSTON

① START

② P

St Govan's Head

O   1 km

O   1 mile

N

26 Bosherston

Fact File

Distance:	18 miles (28.9 km)
Time:	5-6 hours
Maps:	OS Landranger 158 Tenby & surrounding area; OS Outdoor Leisure 36 South Pembrokeshire
Start:	Bosherston car park SM 966947
Nearest Town:	Pembroke
Terrain:	A mix of bridleways, tracks, lanes and quiet roads, through rolling countryside. Muddy in places.
Refreshments:	Bosherston: cafe, inn and shop
Parking:	See Start
Gates:	15
Suitable for:	Those wanting a good mix of off-road and quiet country lane cycling.
Note:	This is another route inspired by a leaflet produced by SPARC and has a good smattering of 'cycle route' waymarking. However, part of this route is closed at times for live firing on Castlemartin Artillery Range. Telephone 01646 661321 for firing times or check the local newspaper.

Along the way

This ride starts from the car park situated close to the famous Bosherston lily ponds, occupying limestone valleys flooded in the 18th century by the owners of the Stackpole Estate. The ponds form the largest area of fresh water in Pembrokeshire and although attractive all year round, they are best seen in June when the lilies are in full bloom. The estate is now owned by the National Trust, but the lily ponds are a National Nature Reserve, managed by the Countryside Council for Wales in conjunction with the National Trust.

St Govan's Chapel is a little gem and nestles in a cleft in the towering limestone cliffs, west of St Govan's Head. The restored 11th-century chapel was possibly built on the site of a 5th-century hermit's cell and is reached via a flight of steep stone steps. Legend has it that Sir Gawain spent the life of a hermit in the chapel, following Arthur's death.

That section of the Pembrokeshire Coast Path between St Govan's Chapel and Stack Rocks is one of the few parts of the long-distance path that can be legally cycled. However, the route is closed when firing is in progress on the Castlemartin Artillery Range. So, look out for the red flags and warning signs. Furthermore, do stay on the bridleway and do not handle any hardware you find!

Along the cliff section there are many dramatic coastal landforms, such as Huntsman's Leap. The story goes that a fellow on horseback successfully leaped over this deep cleft in the cliffs, only to die of a heart attack when he looked back at what he had done! But the most impressive sight is close to the point where the route turns inland to cross the centre of Castlemartin Range. The Green Bridge of Wales is a spectacular natural arch and along with Elegug Stacks and other features on this section of the coast, is well-known among those interested in geology. The stacks are also of interest to ornithologists for they are the nesting place of large numbers of guillemots: 'eligug' or 'heligog' is a Welsh word meaning 'guillemot'.

Between Stack Rocks and Warren is the isolated and restored Flimston Chapel—all that really remains of Flimston since the military took this land out of agricultural production in order to enact war games—and the site of an ancient roadside cross.

In Warren stands a restored ancient cross, whilst at Dry Burrows, north-east of the village, the route heads past a host of Bronze Age tumuli, the finest group of barrows in south-west Wales. A little off-route are two Bronze Age standing stones, the Devil's Quoit and Harold's Stone near Sampson Cross. The Devil's Quoit is one of the three 'dancing stones' of Stackpole and one of three stones called the Devil's Quoit in Pembrokeshire. The nearby Harold's Stone also shares both distinctions. It is said that once a year the three dancing stones meet at Saxon's Ford to drink and dance. The devil sits on one, playing a flute, while witches dance around them. Some say this is done on Midsummer's Eve, others say 29 December, but all agree that anyone witnessing the event will enjoy great fortune. In addition to the Bronze Age barrows and standing stones, two Iron Age forts occupy the promontories on either side of Flimston Bay, east of Stack Rocks.

The lake situated between Dry Burrows and Orielton Mill is called Decoy Pond and was created to catch ducks in nets, to supply the tables of Orielton House, now a field study centre of the Field Studies Council.

Passing through woods, along cliffs and across fields, it is not surprising that this route offers a wide variety of views and diverse wildlife habitats, making it one of the most varied rides in Pembrokeshire.

Route

1. From the car park, return to the road junction by the church and turn left. Follow this road past the public conveniences, cafe and pub, and at the junction ahead bear right, past the range warning sign, following the sign for St Govan's.
2. A little over a mile further on, having crossed over a cattle grid at the range gate, lies St Govan's Head car park, complete with interpretation board. After having explored the chapel, which is found nestling below the cliff top and is approached via some rough steps by the white star marker, pass through the range gate and head westward on a rough track—punctuated in places by cattle grids and gates—following a line of short, white marker pegs. The surface is grassier and more compact as you approach Stack Rocks car park. The track, which follows the cliff-top, allows you to marvel at the wonderful scenery. There are excellent views of the cliffs and inlets, one being the famous Huntsman's Leap, located approximately 600 yards from the gate.

The section between St Govan's and Stack Rocks is approximately 3¼ miles in length and *en route* you will encounter signs of modern warfare—wrecked tanks, radar posts, etc.—and prehistoric forts.

3. As Stack Rocks car park comes into sight, the track swings right and is abandoned for a turf ride as far as a hunters gate, near a flag pole and warning notice board. Go through the gate and follow the cliff-top, grassy path to the wooden viewing platform from where you may enjoy the best views of the spectacular Green Bridge of Wales and the cliff scenery beyond. Return to the car park and follow the range road in a north-easterly direction, past Flimston. Some 1¾ miles north of Stack Rock, cross the B4319, which effectively defines the northern boundary of the range. Beyond the crossroads, head up a hedge-bound lane to a T-junction, where you turn left into Warren.

4. The handsome church, well worth a brief visit, has an attractive, restored churchyard cross. At the junction beyond the church (note the old AA sign on the farm wall), turn right and head north along the road signposted to Pembroke, crossing straight over the next crossroads before winding down into the valley ahead. At the T-junction turn right, again signposted to Pembroke, cross Stem Bridge and climb up Axton Hill (a sustained pull), beyond which a rolling ride will take you to a T-junction near the Speculation Inn.

5. Here you leave the public road, turning right down a private road—waymarked as a bridleway—crossing over a cattle grid by the side of the old Gate House, where attractive statues top the gateposts. On your left are the ancient burial mounds of Dry Burrows. Near the first pond, the private, surfaced road becomes a good track, which will take you past a second pond and through some attractive woodland, until you come to Orielton Mill.

6. At Orielton Mill, just before the farm buildings, turn left and follow a waymarked green lane north-eastwards for about half a mile, as far as a crossing of trackways near a cottage and by the corner of a walled wood, close to West Orielton. Turn right and follow the track alongside the

wall for the next half a mile or so, passing the romantic ruins of a gate-house tower on your left and a cottage with ecclesiastic-looking windows on your right. Follow the wall as it turns sharp left. Ahead the buildings of East Orielton come into view. Before you arrive at the buildings, turn right at a T-junction of green lanes.

7. At the end of the lane, turn left and follow a quiet road for approximately 600 yards to a wide gateway on your right, by a 'winding road' sign. Head through the gate and along a waymarked bridleway, following the left-hand hedge through a gate and into a short section of green lane. After passing through another gate, follow the right-hand hedge between some farm buildings to reach the road.

8. Turn left and follow the road for some 250 yards, turning right just beyond Yerbeston Cottage. Continue over a cattle grid, along a surfaced farm lane, and through the farmyard. Beyond the farm, follow a rough track which brings you out onto the B4319.

9. After turning left, the B4319 drops steeply down into a valley and climbs even more steeply to the T-junction at the top of the hill. Turn right and follow the narrow winding lane, bounded by high hedges, for about ¾ mile to a second T-junction. Turn right again and head downhill for about ¾ mile to a T-junction by Throstle Mill. Turn right again, signposted to Stackpole and Freshwater East. After approximately 500 yards, you abandon the surfaced road by turning right to follow a waymarked bridleway in a southerly direction.

10. The bridleway follows a green lane up through trees to a T-junction of green lanes, where you turn left. The surface improves as you drop down again, in places over bedrock, to join a minor road at a junction where you head straight on. Continue to a T-junction in Cheriton or Stackpole Elidor, a distance of about ½ mile.

11. Head across the junction and follow the track on your left—not the one by Stackpole Church Hall—past the front of the church and into Cheriton Bottom woods, owned by the National Trust. The track, which follows the valley bottom, alongside a rushing stream and some ponds,

eventually joins a quiet road west of Stackpole village. Turn right and follow the road for approximately 1 mile to a T-junction. Turn left and head along the B4319 for 600 yards or so to the junction by Sampson farm.

12. Take the second left turn, signposted to Bosherston, and follow the road back into the village. The standing stone, the Devil's Quoit, lies in the field on your right by Sampson Cross. As you enter Bosherston, turn left by the church to regain the start of the ride. If you have time, a stroll around the lily ponds is recommended, as is a visit to the cafe in the village.

St Govan's Chapel, Bosherston (Ride 26).

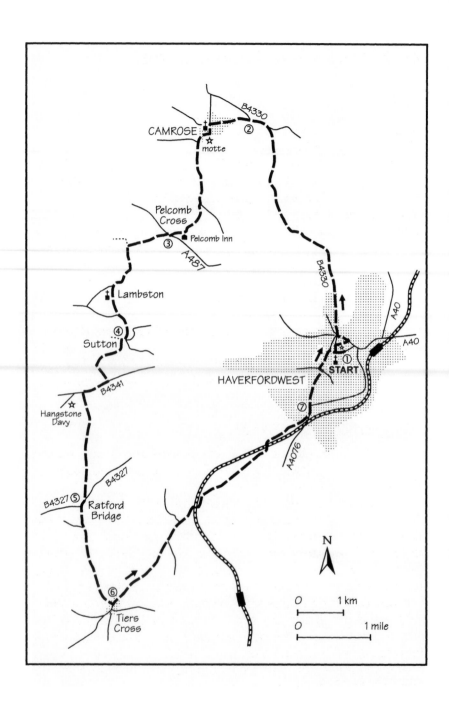

27 Haverfordwest and Camrose

Fact File

Distance:	16 miles (25.7 km)
Time:	4-5 hours
Maps:	OS Landranger 157 St Davids & Haverfordwest; OS Outdoor Leisure 36 South Pembrokeshire
Start:	Haverfordwest Castle SM 953157
Nearest Town:	Haverfordwest
Terrain:	Mainly quiet lanes and minor roads in rolling countryside. Some short, steep sections. Traffic problems on busy roads in Haverfordwest.
Refreshments:	Haverfordwest: everything available
	Pelcomb Cross: Pelcomb Inn
	Tiers Cross: inn
Parking:	Plenty of choice of car parks in Haverfordwest
Suitable for:	Most cyclists, though the busy roads in Haverfordwest deserve great care. Younger riders should be closely supervised in the town.

Along the way

For information relating to Haverfordwest and Camrose, see Ride 19: Haverfordwest and Llawhaden, p. 133 and Ride 25: Wolfscastle and Camrose, p. 167.

The route passes several ancient sites, such as possible Iron Age forts near Lambston and Denant, and the Hangstone Davy standing stone. This stone, a little off-route alongside the B4341 in the direction of Broad Haven, is said to be *either* a Bronze Age stone moved from its original site, *or* a medieval inscribed stone named after an unfortunate farmer, Davy Martin. This poor soul is said to have rested against the stone with a sheep tied over his shoulders, for ease of carrying. The sheep slipped and the rope binding its legs strangled Davy as he was pinned backwards over the rock.

Some evidence of early coal mining is to be found in the area, whilst Tiers Cross, set in a mainly agricultural area but close to Boltonhill Quarry, is a post-19th-century village that grew up around the chapel and crossroads.

Route

1. From the castle entrance head down Castle Street towards the Church of St Martin of Tours with its unusual spire. This is the oldest church in Haverfordwest and is worth visiting. As you reach the churchyard wall, turn right down North Street and follow the one-way system down Holloway to the roundabout. Turn left and continue to the next roundabout (busy at times), which you circle and leave via the quiet B4330, signposted to Croes-goch. Follow the road, flanked by trees and high hedgebanks as it winds up the Western Cleddau valley. At a junction some 3½ miles from Haverfordwest, bear left, signposted to Camrose.
2. Follow the minor road to the centre of the village, turn left opposite the phone box and continue along a lane signposted to Keeston and Pelcomb. Drop down past the old mill, then up to a T-junction, where you go straight on, signposted to Pelcomb. Follow the undulating and winding road to a T-junction, where you turn right, signposted to Pelcomb Cross.
3. At the junction with the A487 near the Pelcomb Inn, some 1¾ miles from Camrose, turn right, then left and head along a lane, signposted to Lambston. At the next junction, turn left, drop down into the valley, across Pelcomb Brook, then climb steeply up to Lambston. Near the Celtic-style church, bear left, signposted to Sutton. At the next junction turn left, signposted to Haverfordwest.
4. At the staggered crossroads in Sutton, turn right, signposted to Broad Haven. This will bring you to a T-junction where you again turn right, then left at the next T-junction, signposted to Tiers Cross.
5. Near Ratford Bridge, some 1¼ miles south of the B4341, turn right, then left at the next two junctions to reach a T-junction at Tiers Cross.
6. At the junction, turn left, signposted to Merlin's Bridge. Beware of traffic at the railway bridge between Tiers Cross

and Merlin's Bridge. At the T-junction near Merlin's Bridge, turn left and follow the A4076, signposted Haverfordwest, to the roundabout.

7. At the roundabout at Merlin's Bridge, take the road signposted to St Davids and town centre. At a second roundabout at the top of the hill, go straight on, again following signs for St Davids and town centre. The route is now downhill and soon becomes one-way as it zigzags towards the river. At the first junction, turn left by Dew Street Newsagents and head along Herbert Street; at the next junction, turn right, signposted to St Davids and town centre, past Perrots Terrace (1850) and an old school, as well as a house with the most amazing cast-iron frontage. Just beyond Bethesda Baptist Chapel, turn second right and head up Church Street and then Castle Street to the start of the route at the castle.

A Welsh Glossary

Visitors may be surprised to find that over much of north Pembrokeshire and elsewhere in Wales, Welsh is spoken as a first language. Welsh place-names dominate north Pembrokeshire but they are also encountered in the south of the county. At first they may prove to be both unpronounceable and incomprehensible. However, unlike English, Welsh is a phonetic language and once you have mastered the sounds of the letters, pronunciation is no problem. Furthermore, place-names are often descriptive of site and include commonly recurring elements. The glossary may help you to a better understanding of their meaning. Also listed below are a few useful and polite greetings.

Pronunciation

a	=	ah
c	=	k (hard)
ch	=	as in the Scottish 'loch'
dd	=	th in 'the'
e	=	eh
f	=	v
ff	=	f
g	=	as in 'go' (hard)
i	=	ee
ll	=	the sound is produced by placing the tongue against the roof of the mouth at the back of the front teeth, and gently blowing
o	=	as in 'port'
th	=	as in 'through'
w	=	often as 'oo'. Cwm (valley) sounds like 'coomb'
y	=	as e in 'the', or as i. Dyffryn (valley) may therefore sound like 'duffrin'.

Glossary

aber	=	estuary, river-mouth or confluence of streams
afon	=	river
bach, fach	=	small
bedd	=	grave
betws	=	chapel or oratory
blaen	=	head of . . .
braich	=	arm
brith	=	speckled
bryn	=	hill
bwlch	=	pass, col
bychan	=	little
cadair	=	chair
cae	=	field
caer	=	fort
cam, gam	=	crooked
capel	=	chapel
carn, carnedd	=	pile of stones
carreg	=	stone
castell	=	castle
cefn	=	ridge
celli, gelli	=	grove
clogwyn	=	cliff
coch	=	red
coed	=	woodland
cors, gors	=	bog
craig	=	rock
crib	=	narrow ridge
croes	=	cross
cwm	=	valley
dinas	=	settlement, fort
dôl, ddôl	=	meadow
drws	=	door
dŵr	=	water
dyffryn	=	valley
eglwys	=	church
esgair	=	ridge
ffordd	=	road

ffynnon	=	well, spring
glan	=	bank, shore
glas, las	=	blue, green
glyn	=	valley
gwastad	=	plain, level ground
gwern	=	marsh, alder
gwyn	=	white
gwynt	=	wind
hafod	=	summer dwelling
hen	=	old
hendre	=	winter dwelling
hir	=	long
isaf, isa	=	lower
llan	=	sacred enclosure, church
llethr	=	slope
llwyd	=	grey
llwyn	=	grove
llyn	=	lake
maen	=	stone
maes	=	field
mawr, fawr	=	big
melin, felin	=	mill
moel, foel	=	bare summit
morfa	=	coastal marsh
mynydd, fynydd	=	mountain
nant	=	brook, stream
newydd	=	new
ogof	=	cave
pant, bant	=	hollow
pen	=	head, top
penrhyn	=	promontory
pentref, pentre	=	village
pistyll	=	spout, cataract
plas	=	mansion
pont, bont	=	bridge
pwll	=	pool
rhaeadr	=	waterfall
rhiw	=	hill
rhos	=	moorland

rhyd	=	ford
sarn	=	paved way, causeway
sych	=	dry
tan	=	under
tir	=	land
traeth	=	beach, shore
tref, tre	=	town, hamlet
tri	=	three
trwyn	=	nose, promontory
twll	=	hole
tŷ	=	house
tyddyn	=	smallholding
uchaf, ucha	=	upper
waun	=	moor
y	=	the, of the
yn	=	in
ynys	=	island
ysgol	=	school, ladder
ystrad	=	valley floor, strath

Some useful and polite greetings to learn:

Bore da (bor-eh-da)	=	Good morning
Prynhawn da	=	Good afternoon
Nos da	=	Good night
Diolch (dee-olch)	=	Thank you
Dim diolch	=	No thank you